# Four Square (4□)
# Writing Method

## for Grades 7-9

Written by Judith S. Gould and Evan Jay Gould

Illustrated by Christina D. Schofield

**Teaching & Learning Company**

1204 Buchanan St., P.O. Box 10
Carthage, IL 62321-0010

# This book belongs to

_____

# Acknowledgments

Thanks to the students, administration and staff of Windy Hill Elementary School and R.M. Paterson Elementary School for piloting the program and believing in it.

Thanks to Mary Burke for starting the "squaring" and having the chutzpa to make us do this.

Thanks to Peter Correa and Barbara Najdzion for technical and artistic support.

Cover photos by Images and More Photography

Pictures © Corel Corporation

Copyright © 1999, Teaching & Learning Company

ISBN No. 1-57310-190-7

Printing No. 9876543

**Teaching & Learning Company**
**1204 Buchanan St., P.O. Box 10**
**Carthage, IL 62321-0010**

# Table of Contents

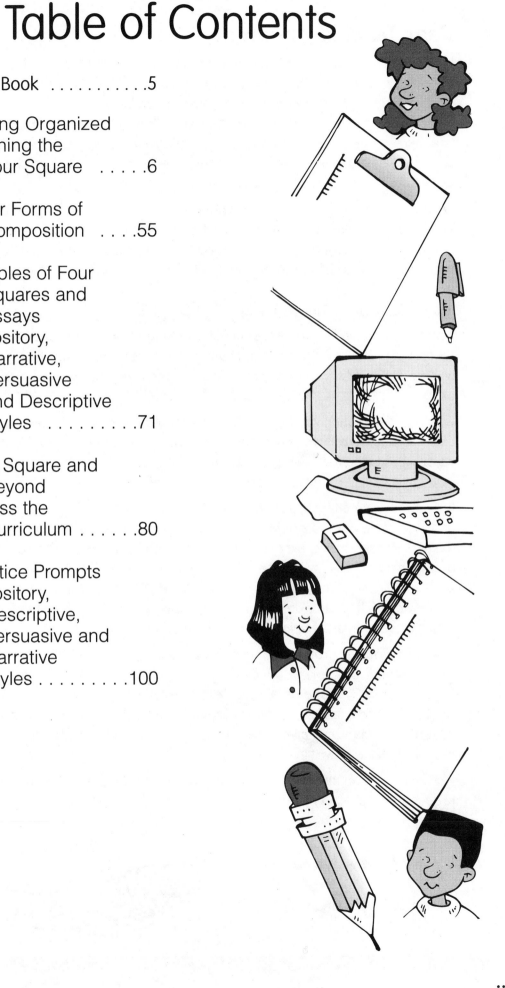

# Dear Teacher or Parent,

In collegiate studies of elementary education, future teachers learn about the importance of writing as a language art. Elementary education students are told that it is a vital form of expression and a communication skill which is required for the work force of the future. Writing is touted as being an interdisciplinary link for classroom teachers to apply almost universally. Today's grammar school teachers are aware of the authentic assessments that students will face, and that the basic language arts skills are vital to their success.

Even while writing has taken a stronger role in the elementary schools, a gap has developed at the primary and secondary levels. High school teachers are quick to point out that students arrive without the skills to take an essay test or to write a term paper. Yet elementary school teachers have been reluctant to abandon current practices.

While this disparity has existed for a long time, it did not escalate to a crisis proportion until states began assessing the writing of their elementary age students. The disturbing results of the initial tests have proven that our children lack fundamental writing skills. Many cannot produce a focused, well-supported and organized composition.

Why don't we teach writing? When we teach children to read, we give them decoding skills to use. When we teach them science, we give them the scientific method. When we teach mathematics, we give them skills and drill specific facts. And yet, we provide little skill instruction for writing but expect results.

In the following chapters we present a method of teaching basic writing skills that are applicable across grade levels and curriculum areas. It can be applied for the narrative, descriptive, expository and persuasive forms of writing. Prewriting and organizational skills will be taught through the use of a graphic organizer. This visual and kinesthetic aid is employed to focus writing, to provide detail and to enhance word choice. It is an excellent aid in preparing students for the demand/prompt draft writing assessments being given throughout the country.

Teaching writing through the use of a graphic organizer empowers students to write with confidence. Gloria Houston in her article, "Learning How Writing Works," for the September 1997 issue of *Writing Teacher* states that "Visual organizers help students to conceptualize, understand and structure a piece of written discourse successfully. Organizers eliminate 'jellyfish writing' and provide coherence and cohesiveness in a piece of writing."

We hope you can use the four square to help teach students writing, thought processes and study practices.

Sincerely,

Judith & Evan

Judith S. and Evan Jay Gould

# How to Use This Book

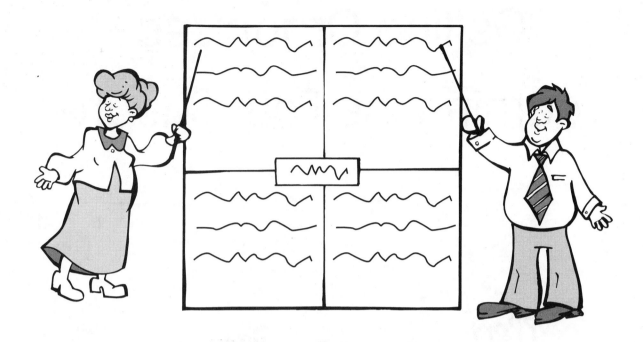

Four square instruction and practice should be incorporated into a writing program that is rich with writing experiences. During the learning of the organizer, students should maintain poetry, shared writing and journal writing activities.

## Section 1
### Learning the Four Square

Each of these steps typically takes about a week of instruction and practice. There should be daily modeling and practice. It is important to remember to keep the writing on the organizer until all steps are complete.

## Section 2
### Other Forms of Composition

This section provides the same step-by-step instruction in organizing a composition for the narrative, descriptive and persuasive styles. It is recommended that these be taught *after* the expository style is learned.

## Section 3
### Samples of Four Square and Essays

This section is for instructor reference and can be used as models for students. There are samples for expository, narrative, descriptive and persuasive writing.

## Section 4
### Going Across the Curriculum

Four square is a tool for organizing, so why not move it out of the composition book and into students' study habits? There are hints for applying four square in other subject areas.

## Section 5
### Practice Prompts

A few prompts to get you started. These are to be used when the entire process has been learned.

# Section 1
# Getting Organized
# Learning the Four Square

Support

Details

Connections

Vivids

# Getting Started Before the 4□

We begin our study of organization and prewriting thought process with a focus on the expository style. There are several reasons for teaching this first. One reason is that students typically find this the most daunting type of writing, and mastery of a difficult form builds confidence for future application. However, more importantly, expository writing on a familiar or personal topic is a classic topic of primary grade discourse and journaling. Students want to tell you about the things they know best and all the reasons they love them. These topics are magically convenient for writing and thought organization practice.

The prewriting organization activities used to prepare students for expository writing are identical to those activities required for the descriptive and persuasive forms, so no duplication of effort is needed to transfer skills. However, the instruction will focus on the expository because it allows for a combination of description and persuasion. Suggestions for teaching the difference between styles is included in a later section of this book.

# Pre 4☐ Activities
## Understanding Relationships

In order to organize writing into topics and subtopics, we first need to explore the ways that things are related. Some words, objects or ideas are broad and can encompass other ideas. Beneath these broad words, objects or ideas we can give examples, definitions or subcategories. Before students can develop main idea and supporting detail, they must understand that the subordination of one idea to another is natural and something they have observed in their world.

Provide multiple examples of this relationship's practice. Students can be challenged to think of as many subtopics to an idea as possible, using cereal brands; rock bands; football, baseball, soccer or hockey teams; television programs or any other familiar and comfortable topic. We want students to feel like this is a "game" and to achieve immediate success in writing instruction.

Reproducible worksheets are provided on pages 9-10 for practicing this important concept.

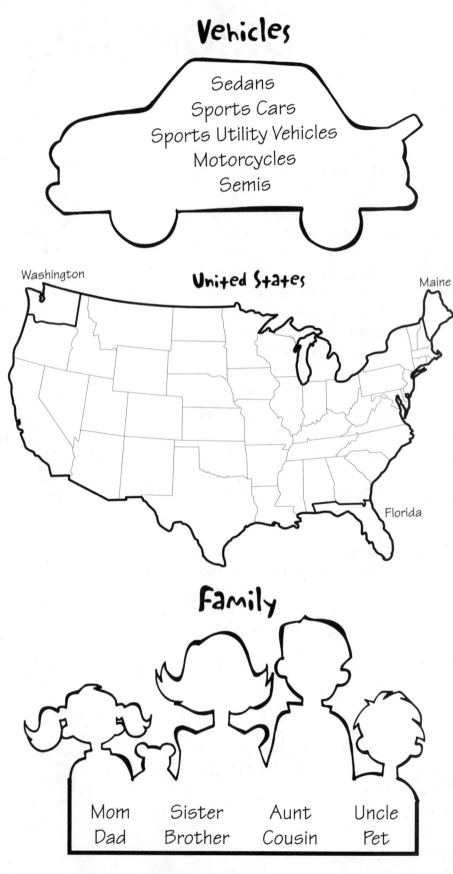

Vehicles

Sedans
Sports Cars
Sports Utility Vehicles
Motorcycles
Semis

Washington    United States    Maine

Florida

Family

| Mom | Sister | Aunt | Uncle |
| Dad | Brother | Cousin | Pet |

# Understanding Relationships

*Directions:* Fill in the lines beneath the topic with three items that belong as subtopics.

People

Birds

_____
_____
_____

_____
_____
_____

Things
to Drink

Subjects

_____
_____
_____

_____
_____
_____

# Understanding Relationships

*Directions:* Fill in the lines beneath the topic with three items that belong as subtopics.

Fruit

_____
_____
_____

Animals

_____
_____
_____

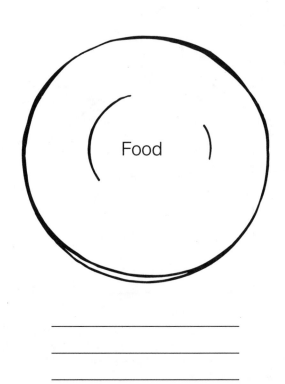

Food

_____
_____
_____

Sports

_____
_____
_____

# Step 1

4 □

## Brainstorming Three Supporting Ideas and Writing a Concluding Sentence

In this step we move our brainstorming activity onto the four square format. We will continue our practice in understanding the relationships between ideas. The main, broad or general idea is placed in the center box of the four square (box 1). The top two boxes (2 and 3) are each used for an example, detail or definition of the central idea in box 1. The lower left (box 4) is used for a supporting example or detail as well. The remaining box, lower right (box 5), will be employed to build a summary or concluding sentence. In practice this is referred to as the "wrap-up" sentence because it encompasses all the ideas developed in the four square in the form of a series sentence.

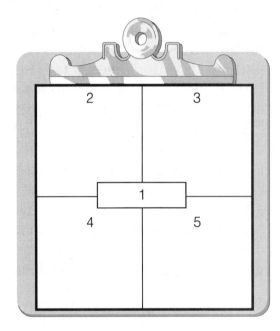

While introducing the series sentence on instruction this early may cause technical difficulties, the importance of the wrap-up sentence cannot be understated. This all-encompassing sentence is the basis for future development of introductory and concluding paragraphs. Indeed, the wrap-up is truly the statement of the three-pronged thesis for a thesis and development paper. Just remind students of the need for commas in the serial sentence and get beyond the technical. **Throughout four square instruction, spelling and most technical matters are deemphasized.** Our goal is to GET STUDENTS TO THINK!

When this stage is first done with students, it is helpful to point out the similarities between the basic four square and the preschool game "one of these things is not like the other" as played on television's *Sesame Street*. Remind students that the central topic is the important one. All other boxes touch the middle one, so we must stay close to it.

The brainstorming should be an engaging challenge to students, encouraging even reluctant writers to participate!

It is recommended that students practice this very basic four square repeatedly. Whole class modeling and cooperative writing can be used. Small group work is also very effective in these early stages of instruction on the organizer. The basic four square provided on page 13 can be duplicated on a transparency for an overhead projector or opaque machine. Each group draws a topic "out of a bag" and the recorder writes it in the center box of the transparency with a wet-erase pen. The group then completes the four square cooperatively. The use of groups removes any intimidation and also promotes the idea that the four square is a friendly, game-like approach to writing. Teams may even race one another. Also, students enjoy writing on the transparencies and placing them on the machine!

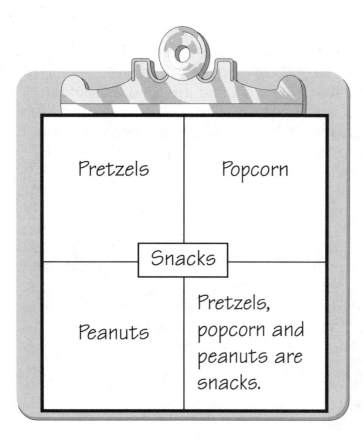

At this stage, students will be happy to be reminded that thus far you have asked them to write only one sentence!

(Reproducible workbook practice pages for this stage follow the transparency reproducible on pages 14 and 15.)

*This example of a basic four square shows the relationships between the main idea–"snacks"–and the three sub-ideas–pretzels, popcorn and peanuts.*

# Group: _____

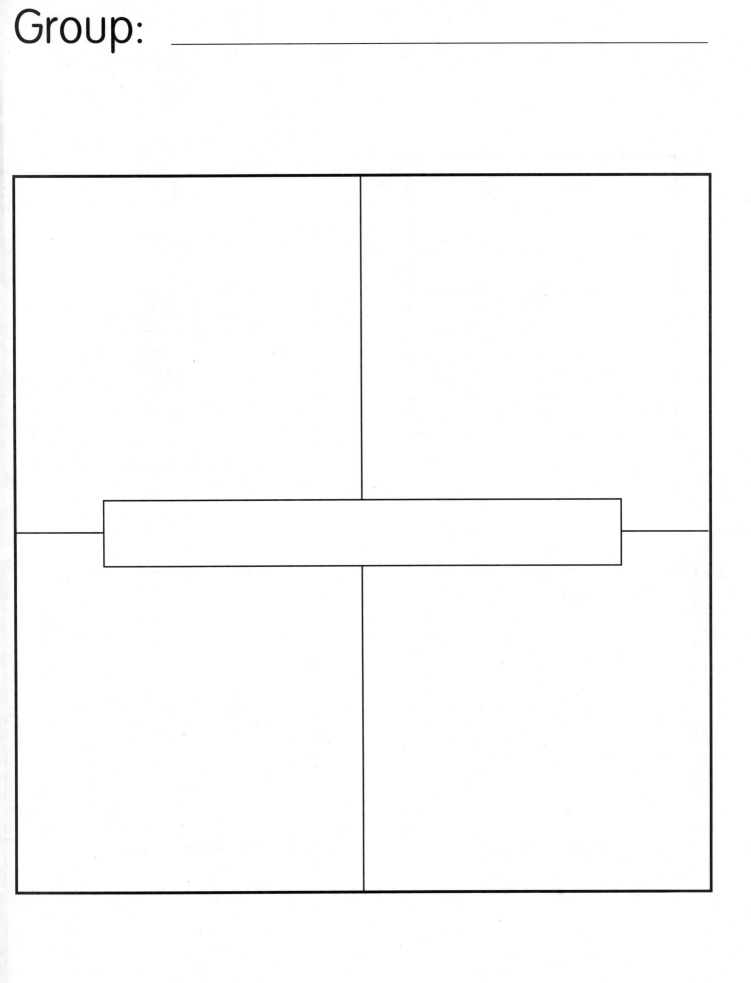

Name _____

Directions:  Complete the four square with one item in each box and a wrap-up sentence.

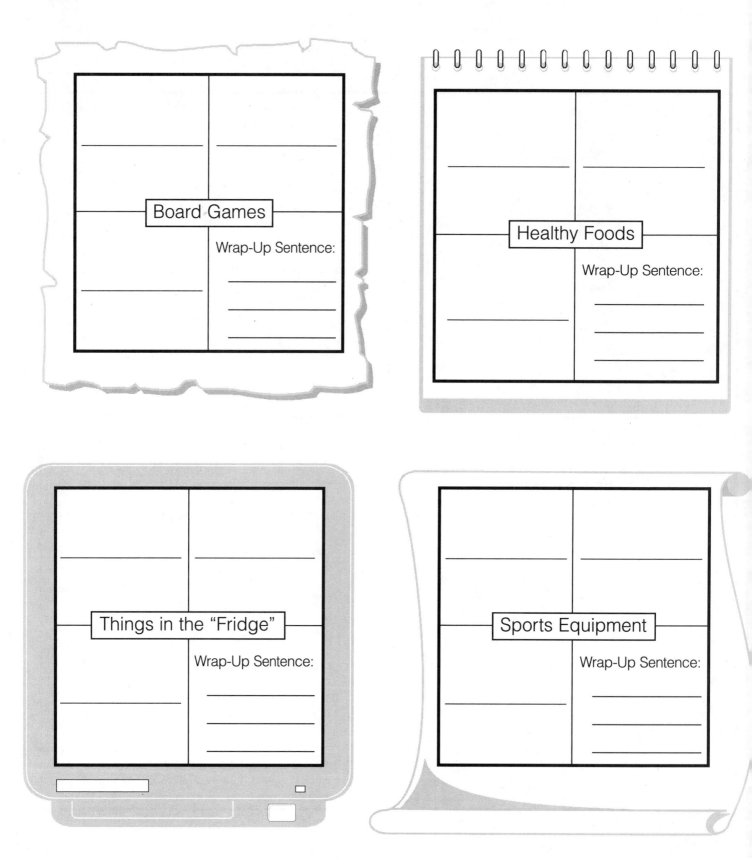

Board Games

Wrap-Up Sentence:

_____

_____

_____

Healthy Foods

Wrap-Up Sentence:

_____

_____

_____

Things in the "Fridge"

Wrap-Up Sentence:

_____

_____

_____

Sports Equipment

Wrap-Up Sentence:

_____

_____

_____

Name _____

*Directions: Complete the four square with one item in each box and a wrap-up sentence.*

Clothing

Wrap-Up Sentence:

_____
_____
_____

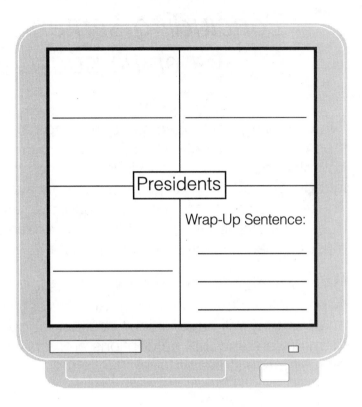

Presidents

Wrap-Up Sentence:

_____
_____
_____

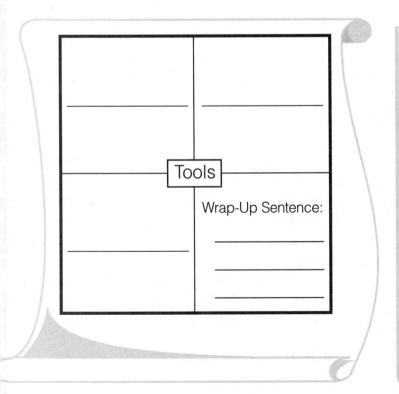

Tools

Wrap-Up Sentence:

_____
_____
_____

School Subjects

Wrap-Up Sentence:

_____
_____
_____

# Three Supporting Ideas and a Concluding Sentence, Using an Expository or Persuasive-Type Prompt

Now the stage has been set for real logical reasoning and persuasion. The next part of step one involves only a small change in the challenge. The center box will now contain a complete sentence. In previous exercises there was only a word or short phrase. The introduction of a complete sentence now alters the requirements for boxes 2, 3 and 4. These boxes must now contain **reasons, examples** or **explanations** that prove box 1 true. These reasons, examples or explanations must all be different from one another and must be real, quantifiable reasons, not merely matters of opinion.

Being egocentric, children may not easily identify the distinction between fact and opinion. If they believe that "fun," "cool" and "awesome" are quantifiable and different from one another, they will have difficulty building a good persuasive or expository piece. To help them understand that perceptions are very different and that an opinion is not reliable, start by telling two stories.

**Story 1**

Teacher: I have just heard a great song. It is cool, awesome and great. Do you want to hear it?

Students: (shouting) Yeah!

Teacher: Great. I didn't know you were into opera!

*Point out that opera is cool, awesome and great to you, but you may not wish to endure any music that is cool, awesome and great to them.*

**Story 2**

Teacher: I've got a great new food here. It's delicious, wonderful and so tasty.

Students: (if they fall for it a second time) Yeah!

Teacher: Great. I didn't know you kids liked liver.

TLC10190 Copyright © Teaching & Learning Company, Carthage, IL 62321-0010

*To provide continuity from now on, it is recommended that you use the same prompt for introduction of additional stages. The familiarity and predictability of the topic will provide comfort for students while learning additional steps.*

*The "spaghetti and meatballs" example will be used for introduction of future stages of the four square development.*

For further practice in developing strong or persuasive reasons and examples, encourage students to "prove" the prompting sentence. The ubiquitous courtroom drama on television has exposed kids to a great deal of persuasive argument. This can help them relate to the need for quantifiable reasons.

A "Prove It!" reproducible worksheet is provided on page 18 for extra practice on this skill.

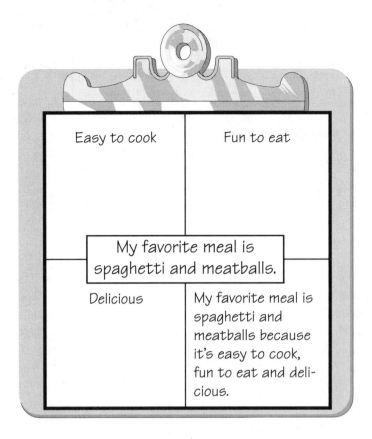

| Easy to cook | Fun to eat |
|---|---|
| My favorite meal is spaghetti and meatballs. | |
| Delicious | My favorite meal is spaghetti and meatballs because it's easy to cook, fun to eat and delicious. |

One area of difficulty that you may encounter at this stage involves the introduction of a conjunction in the wrap-up sentence. *Since, Because* or *Due to* usually work nicely in this situation.

Because the wrap-up is now stringing together different ideas and objects, there is a need to give some attention to the flow of writing in the serial wrap-up sentence.

With modeling and ample group practice (overhead transparency or opaque for sharing), students quickly assimilate the language needed for a nicely flowing wrap-up sentence.

If a student is writing wrap-up sentences without consideration of the flow in the series of ideas, it can be read aloud in a straight monosyllabic monotone deemed the "Tarzan" voice. They quickly understand that the sentence lacks flow when it is spoken in "jungle talk." They will seek to avoid a "Tarzan" sentence when they hear it read aloud.

# Prove It!

*Directions: Circle the two reasons that make the best argument for the sentence. Remember to avoid opinions!*

1. My school is the best in the world.
   a. It's cool
   b. They pay us to attend
   c. I like it
   d. Candy in the lunchroom

2. The beach makes a good vacation.
   a. Awesome
   b. Super
   c. Cool water
   d. Soft sand

3. Pizza is the best food.
   a. It rules
   b. It's inexpensive
   c. It tastes the best
   d. It has all food groups

4. Basketball is a great sport.
   a. Exciting to watch
   b. Fun to play
   c. Mega, mega cool
   d. It's groovy

5. The best book I ever read was _____

   _____.

   Give three good reasons. _____

   _____

   _____

   _____

"Prove It" exercise may be completed orally or reproduced to transparency.

Name _____

Directions: Write a reason, example or explanation in each box to support the main idea sentence in the center box, and write a wrap-up sentence.

It is important to have friends.

My family is very special.

Directions: Write a reason, example or explanation in each box to support the main idea sentence in the center box, and write a wrap-up sentence.

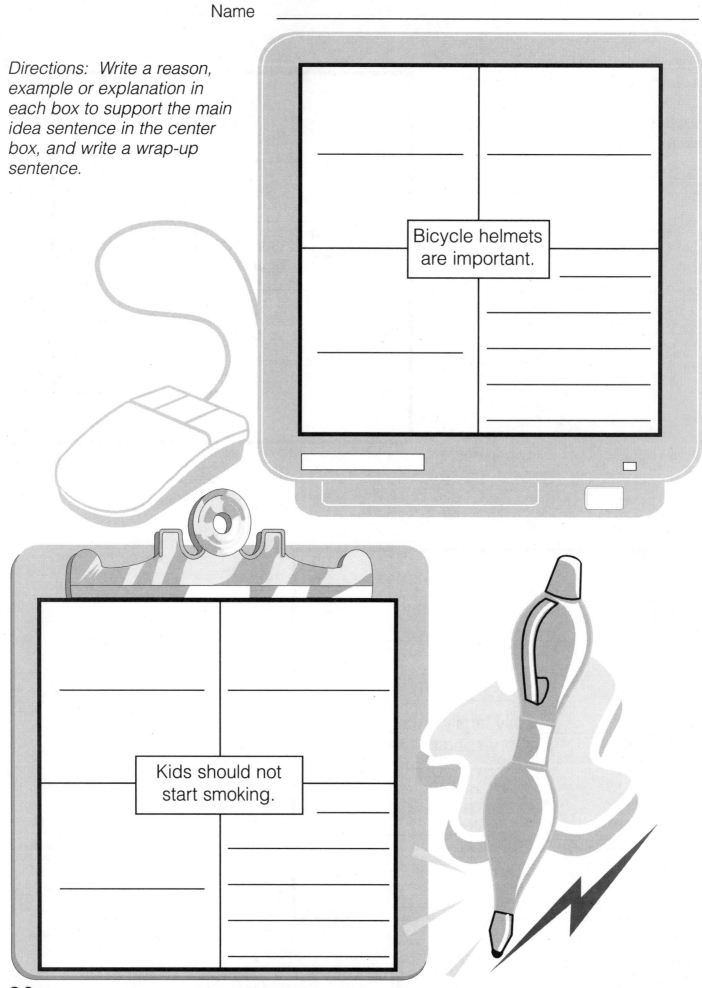

Bicycle helmets are important.

Kids should not start smoking.

# Step 2

## 4☐ + 3
## *Adding Supporting Details*

The reasons, examples or explanations created in the four square stage of organization now need further development. In a sense, boxes 2, 3 and 4 will now be "four squared" independently. These details will be developed later to make up the meat of the paragraphs in the body of the composition. Using the four square to develop these ideas ensures that details are aligned with main ideas, and a topic sentence starts every paragraph.

Students may not be so easily convinced of this need for expansion of their thoughts. One way to point out the need for elaboration is to "read" the story created by four square alone.

| It's easy | It's fun to eat |
|---|---|
| My favorite meal is spaghetti and meatballs. | |
| It's delicious | My favorite meal is spaghetti and meatballs because it's easy, fun to eat and delicious. |

Adding detail and support poses difficulty for some students. Many are not accustomed to elaborating. Writing is not like a multiple-choice examination, and starting their brains may be painful for some kids!

The story created by our example would read as follows:

My favorite meal is spaghetti and meatballs. My favorite meal is spaghetti and meatballs because it's easy. My favorite meal is spaghetti and meatballs because it's fun to eat. My favorite meal is spaghetti and meatballs because it's delicious. My favorite meal is spaghetti and meatballs because it's easy, fun to eat and delicious.

If read orally, the students will identify the repetition and need for detail to enhance the story.

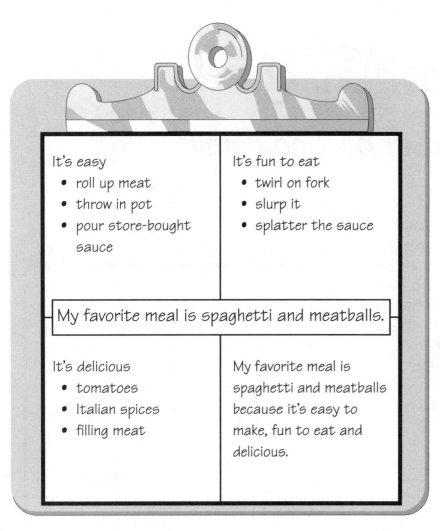

It's easy
- roll up meat
- throw in pot
- pour store-bought sauce

It's fun to eat
- twirl on fork
- slurp it
- splatter the sauce

My favorite meal is spaghetti and meatballs.

It's delicious
- tomatoes
- Italian spices
- filling meat

My favorite meal is spaghetti and meatballs because it's easy to make, fun to eat and delicious.

*Although you have not yet asked students to take their writing off the organizer and into paragraph form, it is valuable to read them the essay in its formation. At this stage this is the essay.*

Occasionally students will need some prompting to elaborate on a subject. For an item in boxes 2, 3 and 4, ask students to prove, clarify or give examples of the word or phrase at the top of the box. "What's so good about it?" or "What's great about this reason/example?" often engages the students' imaginations a bit.

It is important to remind students that *there may not be a repetition* of details from one box to another.

Because of difficulty that some students encounter during this step of instruction, it is recommended that there be ample opportunity for practice. The lessons work well in modeling, group work and individual drills. The overhead transparency group project is terrific at this stage, and each group can have a recorder and a reporter who will read the "story" during sharing.

At this stage you can preview to students that they have done all the hard work of writing a five-paragraph essay!

My favorite meal is spaghetti and meatballs.

My favorite meal is spaghetti and meatballs because it's easy. You simply roll up the meat, then throw it in the pot and pour on the store-bought sauce.

My favorite meal is spaghetti and meatballs because it's fun to eat. I like to twirl it on my fork. It's fun to slurp. I always splatter the sauce.

My favorite meal is spaghetti and meatballs because it's delicious. I like the taste of tomatoes. The Italian spices are great. The meat is very filling.

My favorite meal is spaghetti and meatballs because it's easy, fun to eat and delicious.

Name _____

Directions: Write a reason, example or explanation in each box to support the main idea sentence in the center box. Then give three details for each and write a wrap-up sentence.

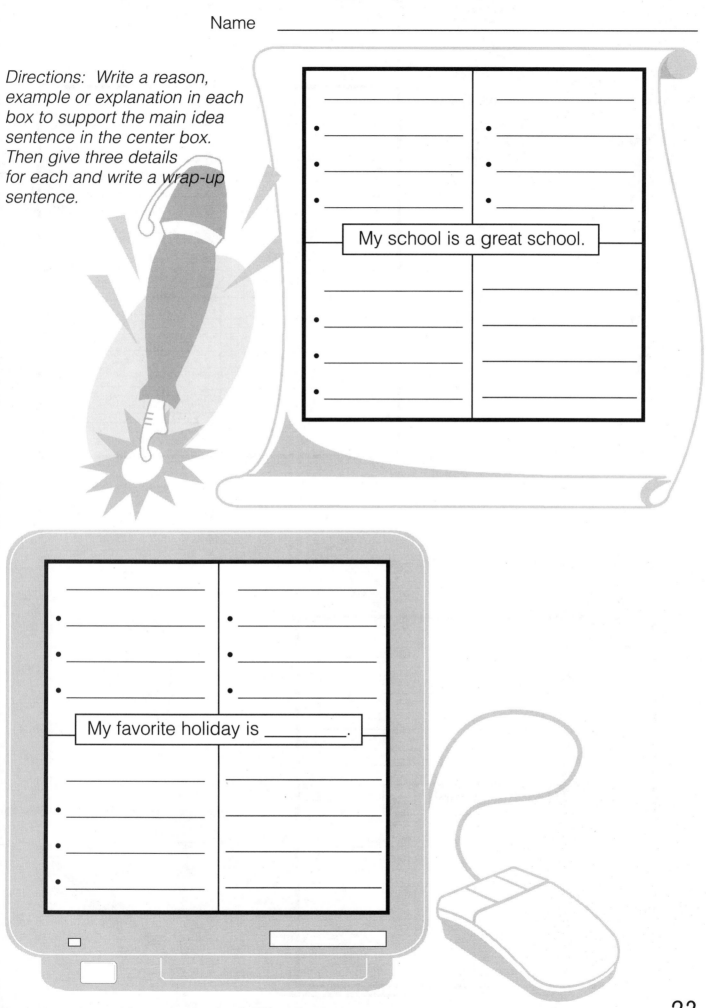

- _____
- _____
- _____

My school is a great school.

- _____
- _____
- _____

- _____
- _____
- _____

My favorite holiday is _____.

- _____
- _____
- _____

Name _____

Directions: Write a reason, example or explanation in each box to support the main idea sentence in the center box. Then give three details for each and write a wrap-up sentence.

When I grow up I'd like to be a _____.

Reading is important.

# Evaluating 4☐ + 3
## *a Checklist for the Teacher*

When the students have achieved a general competency in the four square plus three stage, it is appropriate to give them a "writing test." Students (in this exam) should be given a one-sentence prompt for the center of the four square with approximately 15 minutes to complete it. There is a need for expediting their thoughts because four square is a *prewriting* activity. Even when using an elaborate organizer, we still want students spending most of their writing time on the composition itself.

Below is a checklist that is a useful instrument in evaluating four square plus three.

---

## Evaluating 4☐ + 3

Student Name: _____

|  | Yes | No |
|---|---|---|
| **1.** Are the four square reasons quantifiable and not opinion? | ____ | ____ |
| **2.** Is there repetition of detail? | ____ | ____ |
| **3.** Are the details logical expansion of the reasons? | ____ | ____ |
| **4.** Are the details quantifiable or factual and free of opinion? | ____ | ____ |
| **5.** Are there gross mechanical problems in the wrap-up sentence? | ____ | ____ |

---

# Step 3

# 4□ + 3 + C

## adding Connecting Words
## to Provide Transition Between Thoughts

By now students are developing their thesis (box 1) into three reasons, examples or explanations (boxes 2, 3 and 4) and supporting elaboration. These ideas should be different from one another. These differences necessitate the use of transitions between ideas.

Transition words, or as the formula calls them CONNECTING words, can bridge the gap between ideas. If there are two similar ideas, there is an appropriate connecting word to link them. If there are contrasting ideas, there are words that key us to the difference. These connecting words also provide smooth reading when changing paragraphs. Use of these words is critical to successful writing. In fact, it is so critical that students should not be asked to remember them. Color-code connecting words on wall posters and make them available whenever they write. (See pages 29-31.)

Transition Words

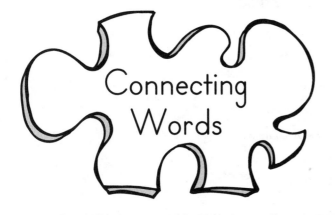

Connecting Words

To introduce the concept of connecting words to students, ask for a show of hands of those who have ever worked a puzzle. Most students can identify a puzzle piece and are familiar with its design. Explain that connecting words are the "little sticking out part" of the puzzle piece; they are words that do the same job as that part. Connecting words hold the different pieces of an essay together.

This explanation lends itself well for the presentation of the connecting word wall posters. To ensure success, the words are color coded. Because box 1 is the beginning of the piece, no color is necessary. Box 2 is colored green (*green* means "go"). Boxes 3 and 4 are yellow to signify moving along cautiously. Box 5 is red, for we are preparing to stop.

Students love choosing connecting words. They absolutely cannot get this stage "wrong" as long as they select the word from the appropriate list. This fosters confidence in students, and this "easy" stage is a break from the more intense brain work required in "+3."

The oral reading of our essay at this stage (Remember, students are writing *only in four square form.*):

My favorite meal is spaghetti and meatballs.

First, my favorite meal is spaghetti and meatballs because it's easy. You simply roll up the meat, then throw it in the pot and pour on the store-bought sauce.

Also, my favorite meal is spaghetti and meatballs because it's fun to eat. I like to twirl it on my fork. It's fun to slurp. I always splatter the sauce.

Third, my favorite meal is spaghetti and meatballs because it's delicious. I like the taste of tomatoes. The Italian spices are great. The meat is very filling.

So you can see, my favorite meal is spaghetti and meatballs because it's easy, fun to eat and delicious.

Provide ample practice with this new step of instruction in modeling group and individual settings.

The following pages are wall posters and workbook pages for this step.

| First | Also |
|---|---|
| It's easy | It's fun to eat |
| • roll up meat | • twirl on fork |
| • throw in pot | • slurp it |
| • pour store-bought sauce | • splatter the sauce |

My favorite meal is spaghetti and meatballs.

| Third | So you can see |
|---|---|
| It's delicious | My favorite meal is spaghetti and meat- |
| • tomatoes | balls because it's easy |
| • Italian spices | to make, fun to eat |
| • filling meat | and delicious. |

*Continue to read aloud all examples as they are completed. This will facilitate the change over to composition.*

# Wall Poster

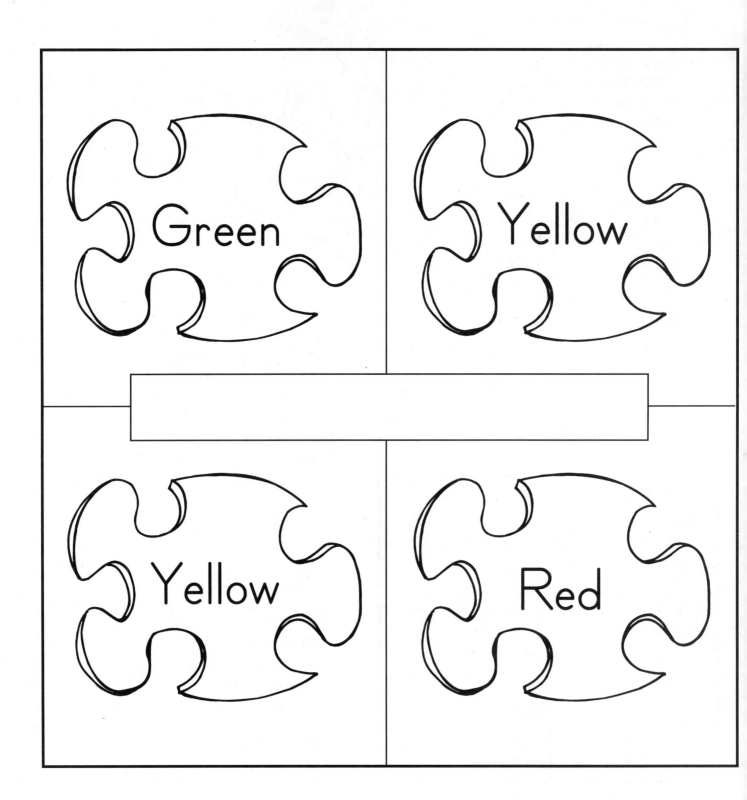

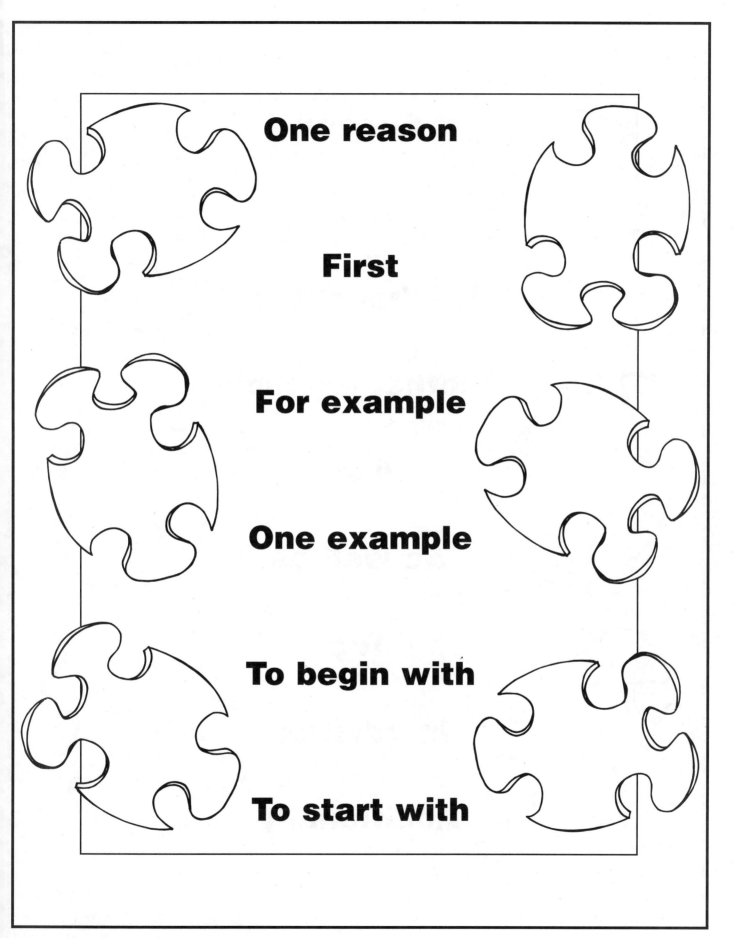

**One reason**

**First**

**For example**

**One example**

**To begin with**

**To start with**

Color the border of this poster green.

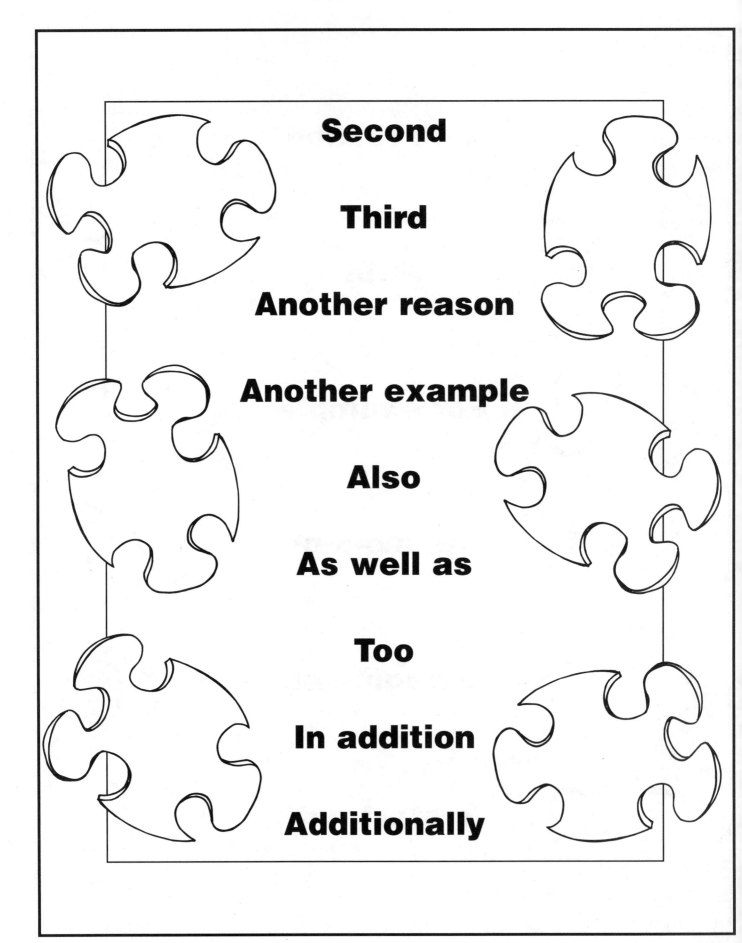

**Second**

**Third**

**Another reason**

**Another example**

**Also**

**As well as**

**Too**

**In addition**

**Additionally**

Color the border of this poster yellow.

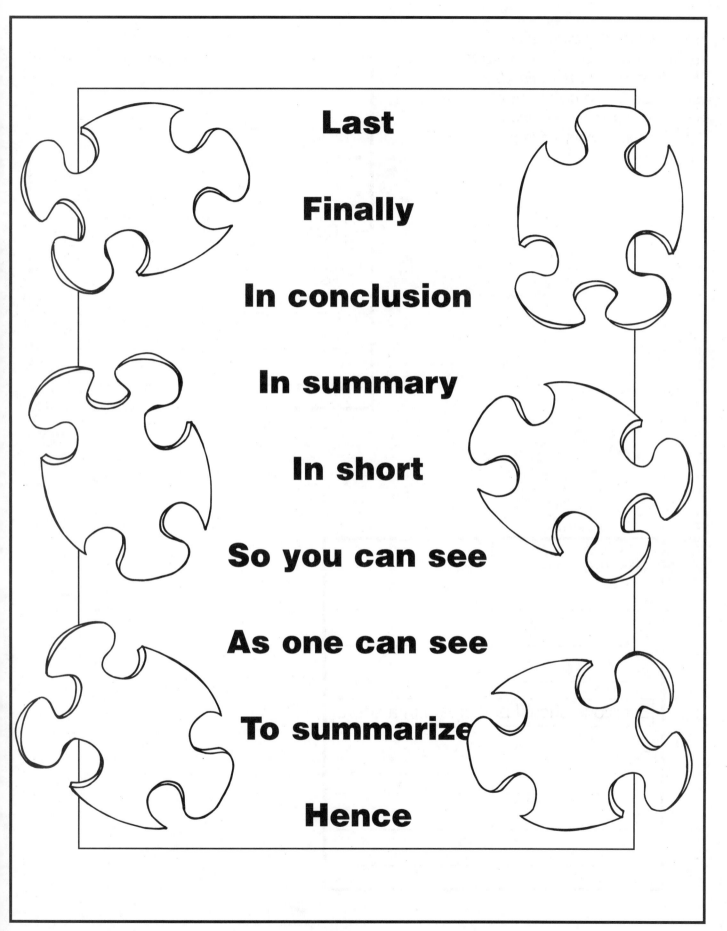

**Last**

**Finally**

**In conclusion**

**In summary**

**In short**

**So you can see**

**As one can see**

**To summarize**

**Hence**

Color the border of this poster red.

Directions: Write a reason, example or explanation in each box to support the main idea sentence in the center box. Give three details for each. Then choose connecting words.

Puzzle Piece

- _____
- _____
- _____

Puzzle Piece

- _____
- _____
- _____

Computers are a great invention.

Puzzle Piece

- _____
- _____
- _____

Puzzle Piece

_____

_____

_____

Puzzle Piece

- _____
- _____
- _____

Puzzle Piece

- _____
- _____
- _____

Everyone should participate in a sport.

Puzzle Piece

- _____
- _____
- _____

Puzzle Piece

_____

_____

_____

Name _____

*Directions: Write a reason, example or explanation in each box to support the main idea sentence in the center box. Give three details for each. Then choose connecting words.*

Puzzle Piece

- _____
- _____
- _____

Puzzle Piece

- _____
- _____
- _____

My home state is the best in the U.S.

Puzzle Piece

- _____
- _____
- _____

Puzzle Piece

- _____
- _____
- _____

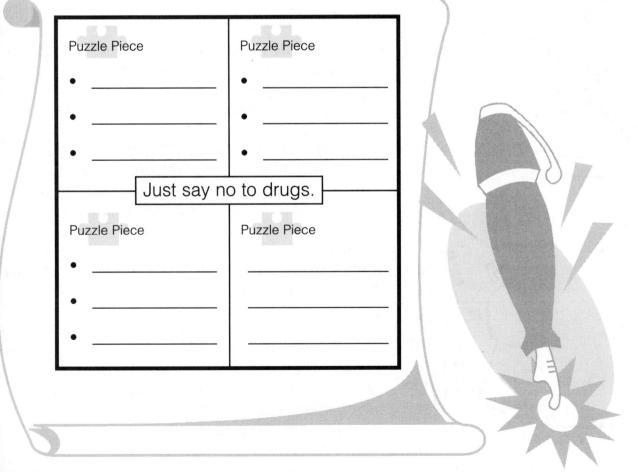

Puzzle Piece

- _____
- _____
- _____

Puzzle Piece

- _____
- _____
- _____

Just say no to drugs.

Puzzle Piece

- _____
- _____
- _____

Puzzle Piece

- _____
- _____
- _____

# Step 4

# $4\square + 3 + C + V$

## Incorporating Vivid Language into Writing

Thus far instruction on the four square organizer has had the goal of building focus, organization and supporting detail into students' writing. This fourth step of instruction begins to assist the writer in developing a style and to use writing as a craft.

Writing with vivid language is achieved by careful, specific word choice. Sensory experiences are an excellent means of providing a vivid expression of thought. Vivid language in writing lets us know what the writer sees, hears, feels, smells and tastes. Vivid language is also heavily involved with the emotional state of the writer.

To explain the need for vivid language, students can be drawn to a favorite medium–television. If you want to explain everything that happened on a particular program that night, you can say there was a "really cool car chase" on a favorite detective show. Or you can say, "There was a detective show where this guy was chasing a '97 red Camaro at high speed up and down the hills of San Francisco. They went squealing past rows of tall, brown apartment buildings. The police car screeched around a corner and whacked into a mailbox. Then the police slammed into a trolley car and, boom, it went up in flames. Meanwhile the bad guys zipped across the Golden Gate until they lost control of their Camaro. The tires were screaming. Then they went silently over the edge until their demise in a tiny splash in the gleaming blue waters below." Ask students in which interpretation is the more vivid description. In which can you picture the action?

To encourage the use of vivid language, students need to be probed. When applying a vivid word to a particular detail, you need to ask students some questions. For instance, if your detail states "a pepperoni pizza," ask students: How does the pizza look? How does it taste? What do you hear? How does it feel? How does it smell? What are your emotions at the particular moment you encounter the pizza? The answers to these questions clarify the composition for the potential reader by giving us more of the picture that the writer "sees" in the mind's eye.

Vivid language writing is not developed overnight, but there are certain techniques that can be employed to encourage its growth. Students can build "Like What?" lists. For instance, a certain attribute may be overused and not provide a vivid enough picture for the reader. The "Like What?" list can be used to give alternate word choices for the writer. It is also an easy way to get students to include a literary device–simile or metaphor.

The "Like What?" exercise can be used to produce some ready references to help writers avoid using jaded language to describe objects or events. Students can generate lists from brainstorming or thesaurus use and post them in a word wall reference area for writers.

*You may need to remind students to not get **carried away** with this. They could develop like fever!*

| Cold | Good | Blue |
|------|------|------|
| ice | as gold | the ocean |
| Alaska | whipped cream on hot cocoa | the sky |
| Grandma's hands | air conditioning in the summer | an angel's eyes |
| a soda can | | a blueberry |

A "Like What?" reproducible is on page 38 so that you can start producing those lists.

On page 37 is a vivid words poster which reminds student writers to engage their five-senses-plus-one when providing vivid language.

*Continue to read aloud all examples as they are completed. This will facilitate the change over to composition.*

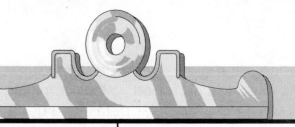

| First | Also |
|---|---|
| **It's easy** | **It's fun to eat** |
| • **roll up meat**<br>golf balls | • **twirl on fork**<br>looks like a twister |
| • **throw in pot**<br>huge cauldron-size | • **slurp it**<br>loud smacking noise |
| • **pour store-bought sauce**<br>Mama someone or other | • **splatter the sauce**<br>like an explosion |

**My favorite meal is spaghetti and meatballs.**

| Third | So you can see |
|---|---|
| **It's delicious** | My favorite meal is spaghetti and meat-balls because it's easy to make, fun to eat and delicious. |
| • **tomatoes**<br>red and tangy | |
| • **Italian spices**<br>zippy garlic | |
| • **filling meat**<br>like a hamburger | |

The oral reading of our essay at this stage (Remember, students are writing *only in four square form* this far.):

My favorite meal is spaghetti and meatballs.

First, my favorite meal is spaghetti and meatballs because it's easy. You simply roll up the meat into golf ball-sized pieces, then throw it in the pot. I use a huge, cauldron-size pot. Pour on the store-bought sauce. My favorite brand is Mama someone or other.

Also, my favorite meal is spaghetti and meatballs because it's fun to eat. I like to twirl it on my fork. It looks just like a twister. It's fun to slurp because it makes a loud smacking noise. I always splatter the sauce. When I'm done, it looks like an explosion.

Third, my favorite meal is spaghetti and meatballs because it's delicious. I like the tangy taste of red tomatoes. The Italian spices are great, especially the zippy garlic. The meat is very filling, like a hamburger.

So you can see, my favorite meal is spaghetti and meatballs because it's easy, fun to eat and delicious.

Pages 37-40 are wall posters and workbook pages for this step.

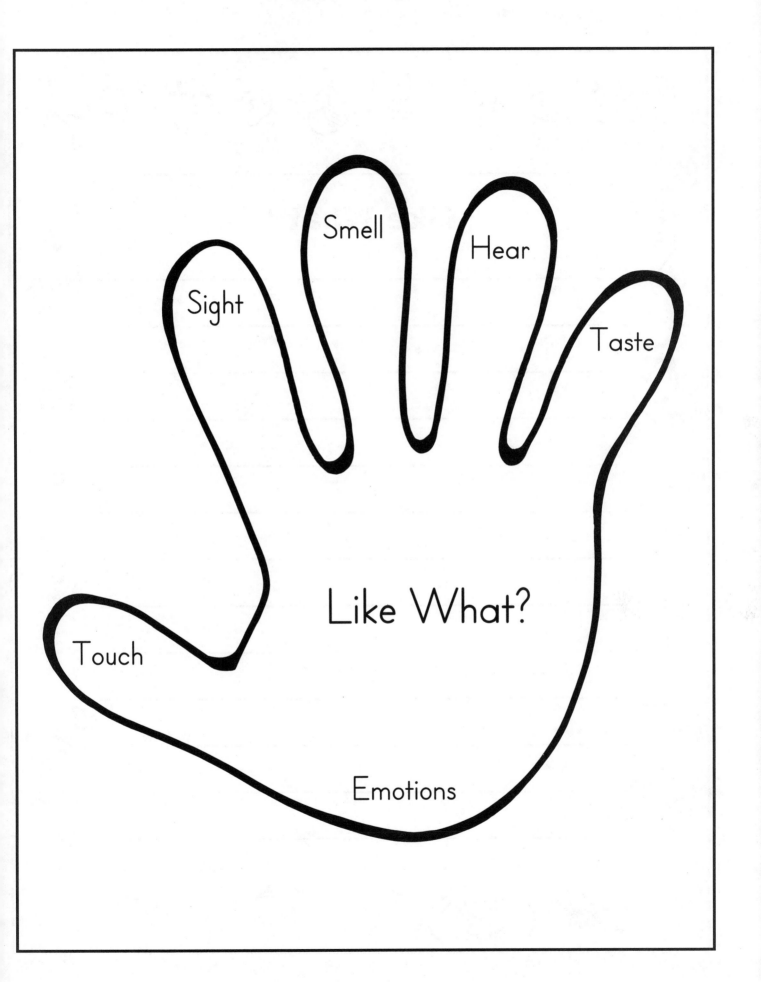

Smell

Sight

Hear

Taste

Like What?

Touch

Emotions

**Vivid Words Poster**

# Like What?

Name _____

Directions: Write a reason, example or explanation in each box to support the main idea sentence in the center box. Give three details for each. Then choose connecting words. Supply one vivid for each detail and circle it.

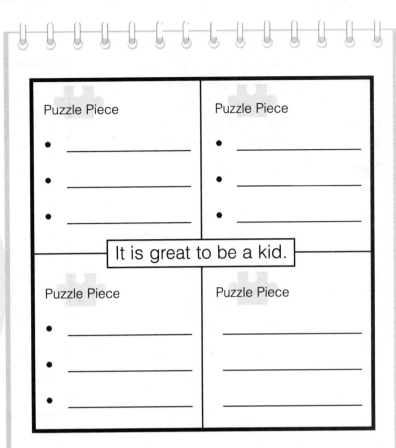

Puzzle Piece
- _____
- _____
- _____

Puzzle Piece
- _____
- _____
- _____

It is great to be a kid.

Puzzle Piece
- _____
- _____
- _____

Puzzle Piece
_____
_____
_____

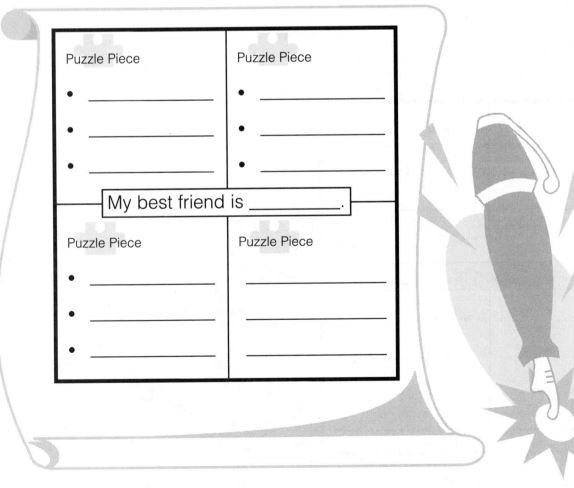

Puzzle Piece
- _____
- _____
- _____

Puzzle Piece
- _____
- _____
- _____

My best friend is _____.

Puzzle Piece
- _____
- _____
- _____

Puzzle Piece
_____
_____
_____

Name _____

Directions: Write a reason, example or explanation in each box to support the main idea sentence in the center box. Give three details for each. Then choose connecting words. Supply one vivid for each detail and circle it.

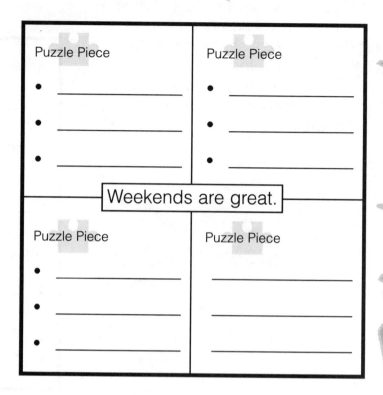

Puzzle Piece
- _____
- _____
- _____

Puzzle Piece
- _____
- _____
- _____

Weekends are great.

Puzzle Piece
- _____
- _____
- _____

Puzzle Piece
_____
_____
_____

Puzzle Piece
- _____
- _____
- _____

Puzzle Piece
- _____
- _____
- _____

My favorite season is _____.

Puzzle Piece
- _____
- _____
- _____

Puzzle Piece
_____
_____
_____

# Evaluating 4☐ + 3 + C + V
## *a Checklist for the Teacher*

Because this is the final stage of instruction on the graphic organizer, it is an appropriate time to evaluate student work. Correcting problems before they get to the composition stage is ideal. Many students resent composing as it is. If we have them correct and rewrite paragraphs of written material, that resentment will deepen. The fixing of a four square is not nearly so daunting a task.

When evaluating 4☐ + 3 + C + V, it is important to look for variety and richness of detail. Also, there should be additional information provided through the use of vivids.

---

# Evaluating 4☐ + 3 + C + V

Student Name: _____

|  | Yes | No |
|---|---|---|
| **1.** Are the four square reasons quantifiable and not opinion? | ____ | ____ |
| **2.** Is there repetition of detail? | ____ | ____ |
| **3.** Are the details logical expansion of the reasons? | ____ | ____ |
| **4.** Are the details quantifiable or factual and free of opinion? | ____ | ____ |
| **5.** Are there gross mechanical problems in the wrap-up sentence? | ____ | ____ |
| **6.** Is there value added information from the vivids? | ____ | ____ |

---

# Rote Instruction

## $4\square + 3 + C + V = 5$ Paragraphs

### *Taking the Writing off the Organizer*

Students have now spent a great deal of time working on the organizer, having never completed the composition phase of the writing process. The oral "story readings" performed with the completed four squares at early stages should have led to the understanding that this was a part of a bigger scheme.

When introducing the concept of moving the information from the four square to the multiple-paragraph essay, it is generally recommended to do a rote lesson. The whole class or group can build a four square together. Then the story is built one sentence at a time. Use chart paper or an overhead transparency with a simulated piece of notebook paper.

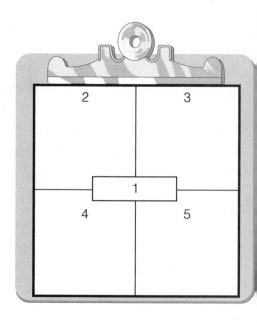

As the composition is being modeled one sentence at a time, students copy it. This "down time" can be used for instant remediation and reminders of the rules of writing in paragraphs. It would seem that no matter how many times a class is reminded to indent, students don't remember until they are reminded personally.

The four square has built in a good self-checking mechanism for sentence building. Since each of boxes 2, 3 and 4 had four items in them, students can be reminded to check for four capital letters and four periods in each of the corresponding paragraphs.

It is important to remind students never to take the shortcut of trying to list all items in each box as one long sentence. Not only is this poor writing practice, but it is bound to be a run-on sentence.

On pages 43-46 are exercises where the four square is given, and students need only make the transfer of skill to composition.

42

Directions: For the given four square, write the information in the five-paragraph format.

| One reason | Also |
|---|---|
| **Sleep In** | **Play Around** |
| • wear pajamas <br> flannel <br> • don't shower <br> until afternoon <br> • lounge around <br> no rushing | • roller blade <br> around neighborhood <br> • board games <br> Monopoly™ <br> • cards <br> Gin Rummy |

Weekends are great.

| As well as | In conclusion |
|---|---|
| **Stay Up Late** | Weekends are great because you can sleep in, play around and stay up late. |
| • sleepovers <br> pillow fights <br> • scary movies <br> big monsters <br> • popcorn <br> buttery | |

Paragraph 1

_____

_____

_____

_____

_____

Paragraph 2

_____

_____

_____

_____

Paragraph 3

_____

_____

_____

_____

Paragraph 4

_____

_____

_____

_____

Paragraph 5

_____

_____

_____

_____

*Did you indent each paragraph (five times)?*
*Do you have your capitals and periods?*
*Did you write from margin to margin?*
*Did you avoid Tarzan sentences?*

44

Name _____

Directions: For the given four square, write the information in the five-paragraph format.

**First**

Honesty

- truthful
  always
- no cheating
  on tests
- confessing
  mistakes

**Second**

Pay Taxes

- on time
  before April 15
- with pride
  patriotism
- every year
  for rest of life

A good citizen has many traits.

**Too**

Follow Laws

- traffic laws
  speed limit
- never steal
  robbery
- never fight
  assault

**Hence**

A good citizen has many traits such as honesty, paying taxes and following laws.

Paragraph 1

_____

_____

_____

_____

_____

_____

Paragraph 2

_____

_____

_____

_____

Paragraph 3

_____

_____

_____

_____

Paragraph 4

_____

_____

_____

_____

Paragraph 5

_____

_____

_____

_____

*Did you indent each paragraph (five times)?*
*Do you have your capitals and periods?*
*Did you write from margin to margin?*
*Did you avoid Tarzan sentences?*

46

# Improving the Introduction Paragraph

## *Writing That Thesis Statement*

The introductory paragraph is perhaps the most important paragraph in a composition. It is the first impression made on the reader. Also, the first paragraph makes a promise. Explain to the students that the first paragraph in a composition sets the tone of the composition in much the same way that a topic sentence sets the theme of the paragraph. The first paragraph will be used to promise the topic of discourse, as well as prepare the reader for the details to come.

The beauty of the four square writing method is that nearly all the troubles faced in composition will be addressed in the organization stage of the writing process. Students at the intermediate level are rarely asked to write a thesis statement and paper or at least they are not asked using that terminology. In the four square, the students have already prepared this information. By writing the wrap-up sentence in box 5 very early in the learning of four square, students have already practiced this skill.

### First Paragraph

**1.** Topic Sentence
*(center of four square)*

**2.** Wrap-Up Sentence
*(without connecting word)*

**3.** Personal/Reflective
Sentence

ACTION!

The first paragraph can now be expanded beyond the one topic sentence. The topic sentence will start the composition. The wrap-up sentence will follow. For the third sentence, the students should write something reflective, thought provoking or a personal feeling. Using this formula gives readers comfort in reading an essay because they will know the topic, be prepared for coming reasoning and know the writer's feeling.

**First**
It's easy
- **roll up the meat**
  golf balls
- **throw in pot**
  huge cauldron-size
- **pour store-bought sauce**
  Mama someone or other

**Also**
It's fun to eat
- **twirl on fork**
  looks like a twister
- **slurp it**
  loud smacking noise
- **splatter the sauce**
  like an explosion

My favorite meal is spaghetti and meatballs.

**Third**
It's delicious
- **tomatoes**
  red and tangy
- **Italian spices**
  zippy garlic
- **filling meat**
  like a burger

So you can see

My favorite meal is spaghetti and meatballs because it's easy to make, fun to eat and delicious.

*Our "spaghetti and meatballs" example*

The first paragraph of our "spaghetti and meatballs" essay:

*My favorite meal is spaghetti and meatballs. It's my favorite because it's easy to make, fun to eat and delicious. I could eat spaghetti and meatballs for dinner every night.*

Pages 49 and 50 are reproducible worksheet practice pages for the introductory paragraph.

Name _____

Directions: Write the first paragraph for each four square. Be sure to write topic, wrap-up and personal sentences.

_____

_____

_____

_____

_____

_____

| | |
|---|---|
| | Thanksgiving is my favorite holiday. |
| | Thanksgiving is my favorite holiday because I see family, eat turkey and watch football. |

| | |
|---|---|
| It is important to get a good education. | |
| | It is important to get a good education so you can get a job, be successful and feel good about yourself. |

_____

_____

_____

_____

_____

_____

_____

Directions: *Write the first paragraph for each four square. Be sure to write topic, wrap-up and personal sentences.*

_____

_____

_____

_____

_____

_____

I enjoy music.

I enjoy music because it's relax-ing, I like to dance and I love to sing.

My favorite teacher is Mrs. Fullam.

My favorite teacher is Mrs. Fullam because she's kind, funny and she helps me learn.

_____

_____

_____

_____

_____

_____

_____

# Improving the Final Paragraph
## Concluding the Composition

Second in importance only to the introductory paragraph, the concluding paragraph in composition carries a great deal of weight. In expository or persuasive writing, this is the writer's final chance to bring home the message to the reader. It is to be used for summary and final emphasis of the main idea.

Using the wrap-up sentence in combination with a "red" connecting word works well in bringing closure to the composition. The recounting of ideas should bring the reader full circle, and the connecting word signifies that this is the composition's end.

At this point of the composition we do not want to add any new information, because it would not be developed. However, after the final wrap-up sentence, it may be appropriate to add a reflective or personal sentence. Encouraging students to end with an exclamatory or declarative sentence usually gets them thinking. It is also an easy way to get them to add variety to sentence structure.

## Final Paragraph

**1.** Wrap-Up Sentence with Connecting Word

**2.** Personal/Reflective Sentence, Question or Exclamation

*This formula is an easy way to conclude the composition. Encourage students to make that personal sentence perky!*

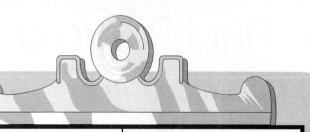

**First**
It's easy
- **roll up the meat**
  golf balls
- **throw in pot**
  huge cauldron-size
- **pour store-bought sauce**
  Mama someone or other

**Also**
It's fun to eat
- **twirl on fork**
  looks like a twister
- **slurp it**
  loud smacking noise
- **splatter the sauce**
  like an explosion

My favorite meal is spaghetti and meatballs.

**Third**
It's delicious
- **tomatoes**
  red and tangy
- **Italian spices**
  zippy garlic
- **filling meat**
  like a hamburger

**So you can see**

My favorite meal is spaghetti and meat-balls because it's easy to make, fun to eat and delicious.

*Our "spaghetti and meatballs" example*

The final paragraph of our "spaghetti and meatballs" essay:

*So you can see, my favorite meal is spaghetti and meatballs because it's easy to make, fun to eat and delicious. I think my mom is making some tonight. Would you like to come over for dinner?*

Pages 53 and 54 are reproducible worksheet practice pages for the concluding paragraph.

THAT'S A WRAP!

52

Name _____

*Directions: Write the final paragraph for each four square. Be sure to include the wrap-up and a personal sentence, question or exclamation.*

_____

_____

_____

_____

_____

_____

_____

_____

| | |
|---|---|
| | |
| My favorite dessert is pie a la mode. | |
| | My favorite dessert is pie a la mode because I like the crust, filling and ice cream. |

| | |
|---|---|
| | |
| It is great to have a brother or a sister. | |
| | It is great to have a brother or sister to keep you company, share your childhood and help you out. |

_____

_____

_____

_____

_____

_____

_____

Directions: Write the final paragraph for each four square. Be
sure to include the wrap-up and a
personal sentence, question or
exclamation.

_____

_____

_____

_____

_____

_____

_____

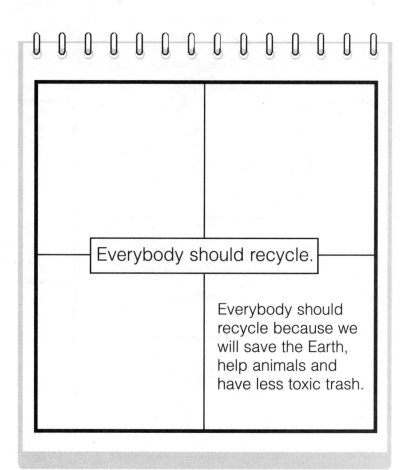

Everybody should recycle.

Everybody should
recycle because we
will save the Earth,
help animals and
have less toxic trash.

It is important to have a goal.

It is important to
have a goal
because it keeps
you focused, gives
you hope and
makes you stronger.

_____

_____

_____

_____

_____

_____

_____

_____

# Section 2
# Other Forms
# of Composition

Expository

Narrative

Persuasive

Descriptive

# The Narrative Style
## Introducing a New Form of Writing

To introduce this new and very different style of writing, you should prepare some kind of an icebreaker activity. Expository writing derives its strength from order, predictability and structure. While these criteria are important in narrative writing, the main purpose of this form is to ENTERTAIN the reader.

An activity that works well to break the ice is the "Timed-write-around-the-room." To start this activity, place a list of approximately 10 words on the board. You can choose any words you like. Seasonal words, names of people and strong verbs are good choices. Ask students to write one sentence using a minimum of two of the words on the list. Once students are done, ERASE THE LIST, or they will use only those words.

Then tell the students, "The sentence on your page is the first sentence of an action and adventure, once-upon-a-time story. Continue writing that story. The objective is to keep writing, no matter what comes into your mind." Though there may be some moans and groans, even reluctant writers like to participate in this game. If possible, you should contribute to the writing, too.

After three minutes have passed (a kitchen timer is recommended), ask that pencils be put down, regardless of where students are in the story. The writers then pass their stories to the left. Each student reads the new story and adds to it, writing for three minutes. This activity is repeated two more times, with the last writer getting about five minutes to write a big ending.

Not only do students enjoy this activity, it shows them what can happen to story writing if they do not plan ahead.

After sharing, it is appropriate to explain the differences between the expository and narrative forms.

## Expository

- Gives information
- States reasons or examples
- Highly structured
- Connecting words a must
- Few quotations

## Narrative

- Entertains
- Has events
- More loosely structured
- Connecting words as needed
- More dialogue

The differences between the two forms can best be exemplified by preparing two basic four squares on a similar prompt. One has reasons, explanations or examples (usually nouns) for boxes 2, 3 and 4. The other has events for these boxes (usually verbs). Which one is telling the entertaining story?

**The narrative four square is the one that shows the ACTION.**

## Expository

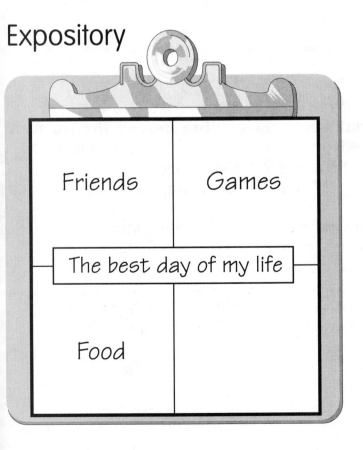

| Friends | Games |
|---------|-------|
| The best day of my life | |
| Food | |

## Narrative

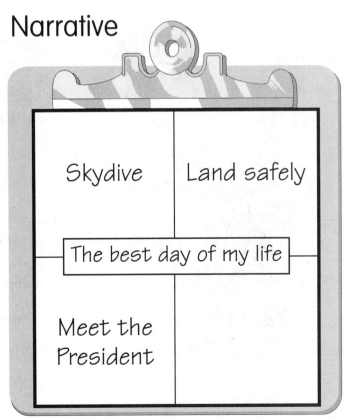

| Skydive | Land safely |
|---------|-------------|
| The best day of my life | |
| Meet the President | |

# 4□ Stage

*narrative*

In the first step of building a narrative four square, students are required to answer the questions Who? What? Where? When? and Why? These questions are aiming at a description of the setting before the problem or action takes place.

*The 4□ stage in a narrative style*

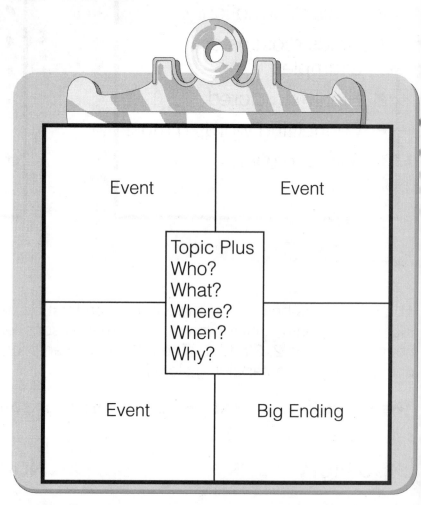

| Event | Event |
|---|---|
| Topic Plus<br>Who?<br>What?<br>Where?<br>When?<br>Why? | |
| Event | Big Ending |

**Who was there *before the action?***
**What were they doing *before the action?***
**Where were they *before the action?***
**When does the story take place?**
**Why are the people there?**

After the setting is established, the writer needs to create events for the story. These events should be ***actions*** with strong, active verbs. If there is no action, there is no narrative story! Box 5 in narrative writing **does not have a wrap-up sentence**. This box is for the outcome or big ending of the story.

Name _____

Directions: Complete the setting, events and ending for the
narrative style four squares.

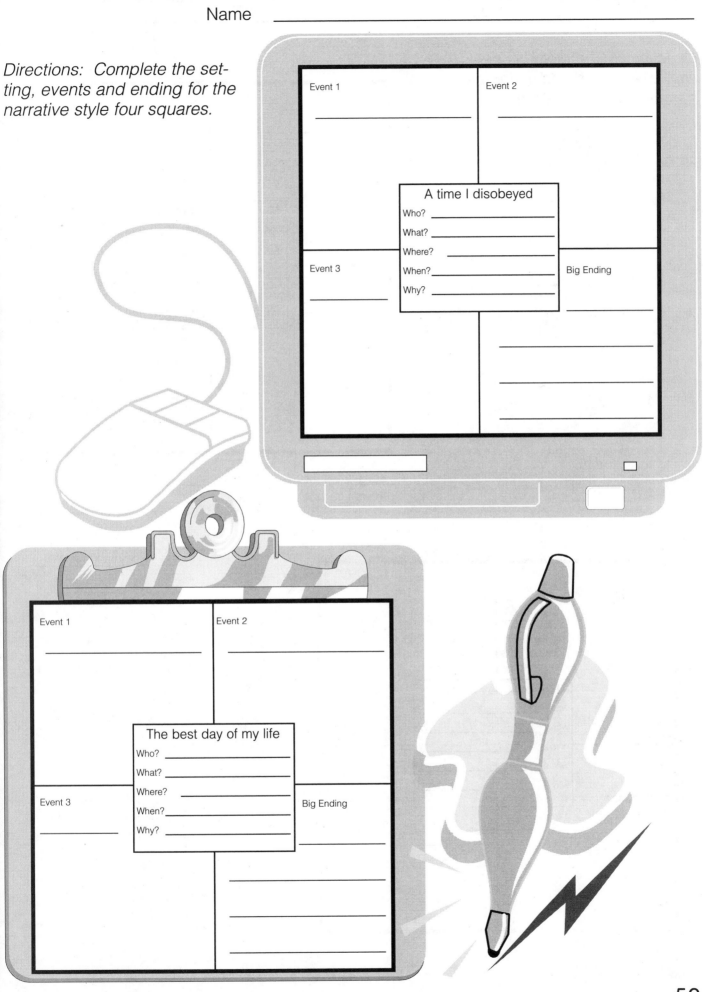

Event 1

_____

Event 2

_____

### A time I disobeyed

Who? _____
What? _____
Where? _____
When? _____
Why? _____

Event 3

_____

Big Ending

_____

_____

_____

Event 1

_____

Event 2

_____

### The best day of my life

Who? _____
What? _____
Where? _____
When? _____
Why? _____

Event 3

_____

Big Ending

_____

_____

_____

Name _____

Directions: Complete the setting, events and ending for the narrative style four squares.

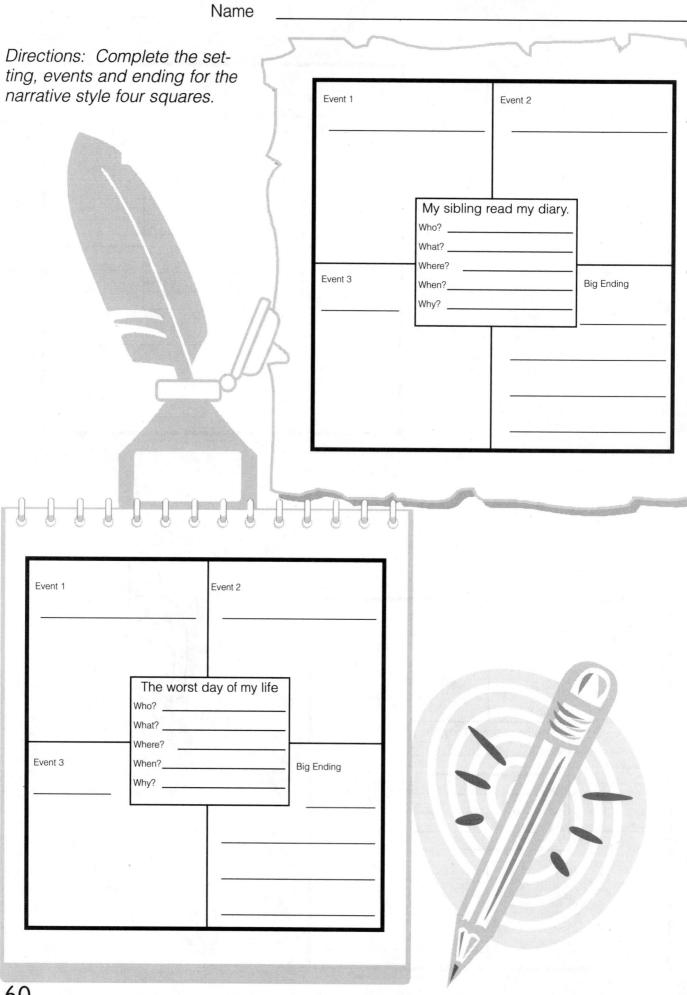

| Event 1 | Event 2 |
|---|---|
| _____ | _____ |

**My sibling read my diary.**
Who? _____
What? _____
Where? _____
When? _____
Why? _____

| Event 3 | Big Ending |
|---|---|
| _____ | _____ |
| | _____ |
| | _____ |

| Event 1 | Event 2 |
|---|---|
| _____ | _____ |

**The worst day of my life**
Who? _____
What? _____
Where? _____
When? _____
Why? _____

| Event 3 | Big Ending |
|---|---|
| _____ | _____ |
| | _____ |
| | _____ |

# 4☐ + 3 Stage
## *narrative*

The "+3" step in building a narrative four square is quite similar to the expository form. The details provided will help to elaborate on the events in boxes 2, 3 and 4. In the narrative style the details can be thought of as a vehicle to explain "how it happened."

It may be useful to compare the details to a description of a scene on television. If a friend had not watched the show, describe everything that you could see.

Remind students to make themselves aware that each box signifies a new event, and they should not get ahead of themselves. Sometimes kids have the tendency to kill off the main characters in a bloody scene even before the action has truly started.

*The 4☐ + 3 stage in a narrative style*

Name _____

Directions: Complete the setting, events and ending for the narrative style four squares. Then add three details per event.

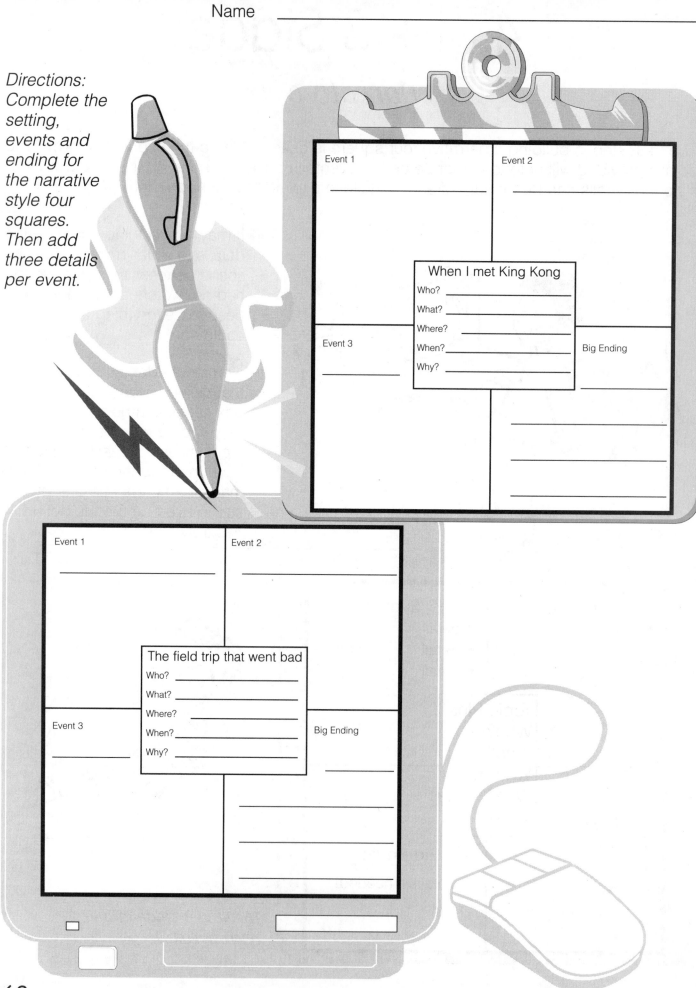

**Event 1**
_____

**Event 2**
_____

**When I met King Kong**
Who? _____
What? _____
Where? _____
When? _____
Why? _____

**Event 3**
_____

**Big Ending**
_____
_____
_____

**Event 1**
_____

**Event 2**
_____

**The field trip that went bad**
Who? _____
What? _____
Where? _____
When? _____
Why? _____

**Event 3**
_____

**Big Ending**
_____
_____
_____

Name _____

*Directions:* Complete the setting, events and ending for the narrative style four squares. Then add three details per event.

| Event 1 | Event 2 |
|---|---|
| _____ | _____ |

**My unbelievable dream**
Who? _____
What? _____
Where? _____
When? _____
Why? _____

| Event 3 | Big Ending |
|---|---|
| _____ | |
| | _____ |
| | _____ |
| | _____ |

| Event 1 | Event 2 |
|---|---|
| _____ | _____ |

**How I became President**
Who? _____
What? _____
Where? _____
When? _____
Why? _____

| Event 3 | Big Ending |
|---|---|
| _____ | |
| | _____ |
| | _____ |
| | _____ |

# 4□ + 3 + C Stage
## *narrative*

In the narrative composition, the use of connecting words is at the discretion of the writer. The words used to connect ideas most often in narrative writing are "time connectors." These are employed to show the time relationship between events that occurred. They generally have a dramatic effect. In one story, it may be meaningful if something happens IMMEDIATELY. In another story if something happens 10 YEARS LATER it may be equally shocking.

*The 4□ + 3 + C stage in a narrative style*

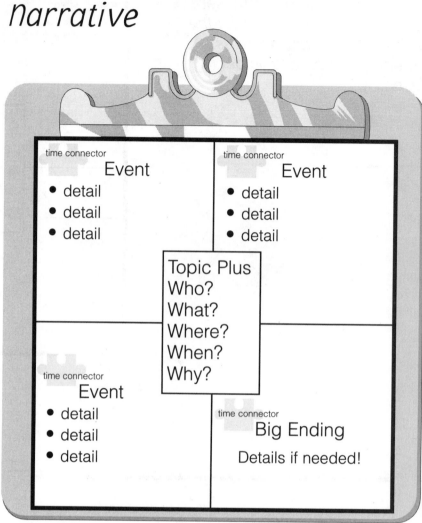

time connector
### Event
- detail
- detail
- detail

time connector
### Event
- detail
- detail
- detail

Topic Plus
Who?
What?
Where?
When?
Why?

time connector
### Event
- detail
- detail
- detail

time connector
### Big Ending
Details if needed!

Because of the flexibility of time in creative writing, it is impossible to "spoon feed" these connecting words as was done with the expository. If they are troubling for the novice writer, they may be omitted.

An incomplete list of time connectors follows.

# Time Connectors

## A very incomplete list

First
Next
Then
Last
After that
Immediately
One (second/hour/minute
/day/year) later
Soon after that
The next day
Later on
In the beginning
In the end
At (give time)
A long time ago
Long after that
Not long after that
Meanwhile
At the same time
That evening
That morning
That afternoon
Today
Yesterday
Tomorrow
Etc.

# 4☐ + 3 + C + V Stage

## *narrative*

Vivids were made especially for narrative writing. When an author creates a situation that is not real and tells a tale of events that never happened, he or she must rely on vivids to make the event seem real. No matter how far-fetched these stories seem to be, the goal of the writer is to make the audience believe.

The writer must bring the reader to the scene by supplying all the sensory information available.

Vivids are even more important in narrative writing.

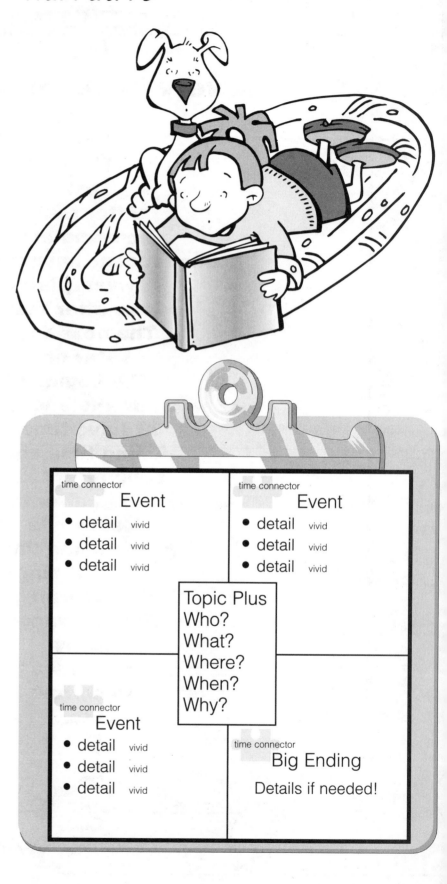

*The 4☐ + 3 + C + V stage in a narrative style*

time connector
### Event
- detail  vivid
- detail  vivid
- detail  vivid

time connector
### Event
- detail  vivid
- detail  vivid
- detail  vivid

Topic Plus
Who?
What?
Where?
When?
Why?

time connector
### Event
- detail  vivid
- detail  vivid
- detail  vivid

time connector
### Big Ending
Details if needed!

Directions: Complete the narrative four square. Remember to start with the setting and events. Then add details and vivids. Time connectors are optional.

Puzzle Piece

- _____
- _____
- _____

Puzzle Piece

- _____
- _____
- _____

The cafeteria lady revenge

Who? _____
What? _____
Where? _____
When? _____
Why? _____

Puzzle Piece

- _____
- _____
- _____

Puzzle Piece

_____
_____

Puzzle Piece

- _____
- _____
- _____

Puzzle Piece

- _____
- _____
- _____

The time I got lost

Who? _____
What? _____
Where? _____
When? _____
Why? _____

Puzzle Piece

- _____
- _____
- _____

Puzzle Piece

_____
_____

Name _____

*Directions: Complete the narrative four square. Remember to start with the setting and events. Then add details and vivids. Time connectors are optional.*

| Puzzle Piece | Puzzle Piece |
| --- | --- |
| • _____ | • _____ |
| • _____ | • _____ |
| • _____ | • _____ |

**The worm in my French fries**

Who? _____
What? _____
Where? _____
When? _____
Why? _____

| Puzzle Piece | Puzzle Piece |
| --- | --- |
| • _____ | _____ |
| • _____ | _____ |
| • _____ | _____ |

| Puzzle Piece | Puzzle Piece |
| --- | --- |
| • _____ | • _____ |
| • _____ | • _____ |
| • _____ | • _____ |

**My teacher became a frog.**

Who? _____
What? _____
Where? _____
When? _____
Why? _____

| Puzzle Piece | Puzzle Piece |
| --- | --- |
| • _____ | _____ |
| • _____ | _____ |
| • _____ | _____ |

# "Hooks" to Be Used with Narrative Writing

## *Several Ways to Engage the Reader from the Start*

The function of the narrative style is to entertain the reader. In doing so, the writer hopes to attract the reader's interest so the reader will want to read the story.

One method of attracting reader interest is the use of a hook. The hook is a one-sentence device placed at the beginning of the story. Hooks are used in an attempt to generate curiosity in the reader.

The hook is to be followed by the setting and event paragraphs, as usual.

## Hooks to Be Used in Narrative Writing

| | |
|---|---|
| The Question | *Have you ever been afraid to fly? Well I was . . .* |
| The Quotation | *"Run and don't look back!" my brother shouted.* |
| Hyperbole | *That pumpkin was as big as a school bus.* |
| Fragments | *Pennies. Pennies everywhere. Far as I could see.* |
| Famous Name or Place | *The Statue of Liberty, there she stood.* |
| Money | *Ten million dollars, and all mine.* |

# The Descriptive and Persuasive Writing Styles

## Going Right or Left of the Expository

The persuasive and descriptive writing forms are organized in a manner very similar to the expository. The scale shown moves from persuasive through expository to descriptive. Because the expository form is a combination of persuasion and descriptive detail, it lies at the midpoint of the scale.

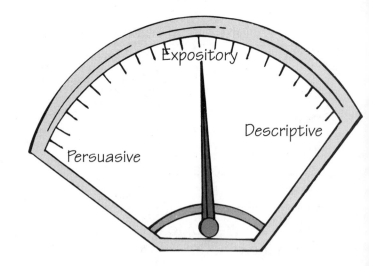

To use four square for the other two styles, a writer needs to be concerned with the difference in the topic sentences for the body paragraphs; the major difference lies in the intent of the information completed in the 4□ + 3 stage.

In the three styles the structure and form are identical. All benefit from the detailed and specific prewriting thought achieved through the use of the four square method.

For examples of four squares and essays in these styles, check the writing examples section.

# Section 3
# Samples of Four Squares and Essays

*Expository, Narrative, Persuasive and Descriptive Styles*

# Expository

### One reason

#### Big bedroom

- room to relax
  big bed

- room for friends
  play with computer

- closet space
  clothes
  sports equipment

### Also

#### Fireplace

- warm
  like a mitten

- crackling
  like my cereal

- smoky smell
  campfire

**My home is a special place.**

### Third

#### My porch

- screened
  no bugs

- relaxing
  listen to birds

- cool
  evening breezes

### In summary

My home is a special place because it has a big bedroom, a fireplace and a porch.

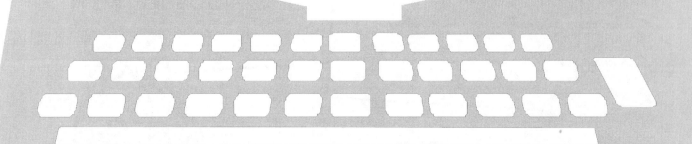

# Expository Essay

My home is a special place. It is special because it has a fireplace, a big bedroom and a porch. It is a wonderful place to live.

One reason my home is special is because I love my big bedroom. I have a big bed I can relax on. There is a lot of room for friends so we can play games on my computer. I need all my closet space for my clothes and sports equipment like my basketball and tennis racket.

Also, my fireplace is wonderful. On chilly nights it keeps me warm as a mitten. I love to listen to the cracking. It sounds like my breakfast cereal! The smoky, woodsy smell reminds me of the days when I go camping.

Third, my home has a terrific porch. The porch is screened, which is lucky for me. I am a bug magnet! My porch is a great place for relaxing. Listening to the birds is a good way to unwind. Even on warm nights the porch is cool because you can enjoy the evening breezes.

In summary, my home is special because it has a big bedroom, a fireplace and a porch. I couldn't imagine living anywhere else.

# Narrative

In the beginning
    Cat food commercial came on
- dancing cats
  top hats
- singing about food
  "meow-yum"
- I said it was
  cute
  laughed

During the commercial
    My cat hissed
- arched his back
  angry
- his hair stood up
  like a porcupine
- loud scream
  ear-splitting

When my cat started talking
Who?    My cat and I
What?    Relaxing
Where?    At home
When?    In the evening
Why?    It had been a long day

Just then
    He started
      talking
- called the commercial
  foolish
  snarled
- said the food was gross
  for dogs
- told me never to buy it again
  I thought it was his favorite

Since that day

He has never spoken again.

I stopped buying that food.

My cat has restrictions on his TV time.

74

TLC10190 Copyright © Teaching & Learning Company, Carthage, IL 62321-0010

# Narrative Essay

One evening I was relaxing at home. My cat and I were watching television. It had been a long day, and I needed some time to wind down.

In the beginning of our favorite show, a commercial came on for a brand of cat food I usually buy. This commercial had adorable little dancing cats. They were wearing black top hats. The cats were also singing about the cat food. "Meow-yum, meow-yum," they sang. I thought it was cute, and I laughed out loud.

During this commercial my cat hissed, which is not something he usually does. He arched his back and looked quite angry. The hair on his back was standing up like porcupine quills. He let out an ear-splitting scream.

Just then he started talking. He called the commercial foolish and snarled at the television. My cat told me that brand of cat food was gross, and it was only good for dogs, which means that it must be pretty bad. Then he told me never to buy it again. I had always thought he liked the stuff!

Since that day my cat has not spoken again. I did stop buying that brand of cat food. But because of his ill-mannered hissing and growling, my cat has had a limit placed on his television time.

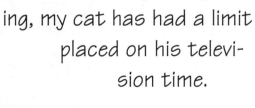

# Persuasive

**One reason**

Relaxation

- stress isn't healthy
  heart attacks
- more time for recreation
  watching TV
- catch up on reading
  good book

**Also**

Family bonding

- better for children
  being loved
- help with homework
  private tutor
- sharing experiences
  everyday life

> The school week should be shortened to three days.

**In addition**

Less use of school buses

- less pollution
  better for air
- less wear on bus
  save money
- less traffic on roads
  fewer accidents

**Hence**

The school week should be shortened to three days so there can be more relaxation and more family bonding, with less use of school buses.

TLC10190 Copyright © Teaching & Learning Company, Carthage, IL 62321-0010

# Persuasive Essay

The school week should be shortened to three days. There is a clear need for relaxation and family bonding. Also, this would cause less use of school buses. The evidence supporting this change is clear.

One reason to shorten the school week is the universal need for relaxation. Students and teachers under stress are experiencing a health risk. It could lead to a heart attack. A shorter week would increase the time allowed for recreational activities such as television viewing. Perhaps more students would read if there were a shorter week. There are many good books available.

Also, the shorter week would allow time for more family bonding. More quality time is better for children who are so in need of love. Parents can take a role in helping their children with homework; they can act as private home tutors. This shortened week may give parents the time they need to share the experience of spending every day with their darling children.

In addition, the shorter week will lessen the use of school buses. Buses are notorious polluters, so giving them two more days off will be better for the air. Less use of the buses means less wear and tear on the vehicles, and this would save taxpayer dollars. Having fewer buses on the road means less traffic, and there would be fewer accidents.

Hence, the school week should be shortened to three days so there can be more relaxation and more family bonding and less use of school buses. What student or teacher could disagree?

# Descriptive

**One reason**

The grass

- green
  as a frog
- manicured
  perfectly cut
- no weeds
  prohibited

**Also**

Memorial Park

- plaques
  delicately engraved
- jerseys
  well-worn
- tattered baseballs
  signed

Yankee Stadium is a beautiful place.

**Too**

The electricity

- always there
  the eyes of the children
- shouting fans
  Tabernacle Choir
- the memory of greatness
  spirits in the air

**As one can see**

Yankee Stadium is a beautiful place because of the grass, Memorial Park and the electricity in the air.

78

# Descriptive Essay

Yankee Stadium is a beautiful place. The beauty can be seen in the grass and Memorial Park, and it can be felt in the electricity in the air. I love to visit there.

One reason it is so beautiful is the grass. It is always frog-green. The lawn is manicured and perfectly cut. Weeds are prohibited from entering.

Also, Memorial Park is a special place. One can view the plaques that have been so delicately engraved in remembrance. There are jerseys to view that were well-worn by the greats. They have tattered, old baseballs which have priceless signatures.

The electricity in the air is beautiful, too. It is always there, and you can see it in the eyes of the children visiting. The shouting of the fans sounds like the Mormon Tabernacle Choir to the ears of a baseball lover. One can sense the memory of greatness because their spirits live in the air at Yankee Stadium.

As one can see, Yankee Stadium is a beautiful place because of the grass, Memorial Park and the electricity in the air. You should catch a game today.

# Section 4
# Four Square and Beyond Across the Curriculum

Science

Social Studies

Math

The Arts

# 4□ in the Language Arts Program

## Using Four Square as a Part of the Writing Process

Four square helps students organize their thoughts. Teaching this method will help students become better writers. The four square is an elaborate prewriting activity. It provides much of the material that will be applied in the drafting stage of writing. Four square helps to eliminate common errors that create a need for rewriting. But four square alone is not a writing program.

Students need a variety of activities and approaches to spark their creative writing interest. **Brainstorming** on a topic using a semantic map or sensory web is an activity that can be completed before organizing with the four square. Students may have a shared experience to develop their writing skills. Certainly the use of the four square does not call for an abandonment of hands-on learning.

After initial brainstorming is underway, the four square is a tool for **organizing** that experience. It aligns thoughts and prepares them for a composition.

**Drafting** follows the organizing step. This is the manuscript created by writers that is full of errors that need fixing, changing and sometimes dumping. It is a natural stage of the writing process and certainly not the last. Unfortunately, this is the stage at which most states make their writing assessment. That is why we need to make the most of organization; it can help limit drafting errors.

**Revising and editing** follow drafting. This stage encourages proofreading and making structural changes to a piece where clarification or continuity improvements are needed. A proofreading poster is on page 83 for duplication.

During the editing step, students should be encouraged to consider their word choices and sentence structure. In writing, it is desirable to "get the most bang for your buck" and avoid the use of weak language whenever possible.

One way to do this is the use of adverbs and stronger verbs. To develop this sense, a contest can be played using a sentence with a weak or linking verb. Students can be challenged to write as many strong versions of that sentence as possible.

**Last year I *went* to Miami.**
Last year I *drove* to Miami.
Last year I *swam* to Miami.
Last year I *roller bladed* to Miami.
Last year I *hopped* to Miami.
Etc.

This is a fun exercise and students can get carried away with it. It works well with linking verbs.

**I am here today.**
I *stand* here today.
I *dance* here today.
I *juggle* here today.
I *back flip* here today.
I *hokey-pokey* here today.
Etc.

A wall poster that has the five senses plus one formula can be placed as a reminder to students about the vivid language stage. A reproducible poster is on page 37.

Finally, students need to **publish**. They should occasionally prepare a composition free of errors and written for others to see. Sharing of published work through anthologies or authors' chairs is wonderful for student self-esteem.

Four square is only one step in this process, but it is a critical one and one often not taught. Given only the sensory web or semantic map, a student will not have a clear direction for composition.

# Punctuation!

## PUNCTUATION

Do all sentences end with marks?
Is there a reason for each mark I used?
Did I use at least one question or exclamation?

## ORGANIZATION

Did I follow my four square?
Do I have good details and vivid words?
Is it neat and organized looking?

## PARAGRAPHING

Do I have at least five paragraphs?
Do I have an introduction and a conclusion?
Do I start my sentences differently?

## SPELLING

Did I sound out problem words?
Did I check a dictionary?
Have I entered the words in my
  spelling dictionary?

# Practical Matters
## Tips on Making the Writing Program Work

### Supplies

To keep students on task and writing, it is important to have the appropriate hardware readily available. A truckload of pencils and paper is appropriate. It may be cost-effective to use a low-grade newsprint for four square preparation and save lined manuscript paper for drafting and rewriting. These supplies should be accessible to students so they can restock without interrupting instruction.

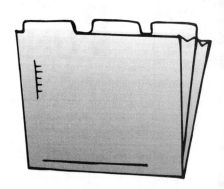

To keep their papers organized, the maintenance of a writing folder is recommended. This folder should have three sections with pockets. The first section in the folder can be used to contain brainstorming activities. The center would hold organizing activities, and the third section would contain compositions. In order to track their work, students should keep a "routing sheet" on the flap of their folder. Each composition has a number, and this number is placed in the upper right-hand corner of every paper generated by the project. The folders should be maintained in a special location in the classroom so they are not lost or destroyed.

You will also need several overhead transparencies with the four square reproducible. Using these with wet-erase markers works quite well for group activities because students' work can be shared very easily.

# Spelling

Spelling is not emphasized throughout four square instruction nor through the writing process. Correct spelling and usage becomes critical in the publishing stage of the process. Because this is when the work is prepared for a reading audience, the conventional spellings must be used.

Spelling is also an issue when students refuse to write because they cannot spell the words and are not motivated to check a dictionary or reference. In these instances, provide them with a conventional spelling under one condition. They must put the spelling in their personal spelling dictionaries (spiral-bound notebooks work well). As the year progresses, each student will have more of the common words in a personal spelling dictionary and will ask less often.

# Conferencing

Practical experience has uncovered that students read almost nothing written on a paper, beyond the grade they achieved. Consequently, it is not a valuable practice to write specific and detailed notes on a paper. The most effective way to aid in student writing growth is the personal conference, even if it is the least time efficient. The trick is how to manage a room of 30-plus students while focusing your attention on one student.

The first requirement is that the others be engaged. Have the class working individually, drafting compositions. This way there should be no inter-student disputes. The conferences can then be called individually. Interruptions will occur, but like anything else, it is a matter of procedure. It is useful to employ an "absolutely no interruptions during conferences" policy. A sign with the message "Not Now" may need to be used during the first few conference sessions. Once students see that you won't be interrupted, they will be less likely to try.

The individual conference is the most valuable lesson a student receives in writing instruction, so don't give up because of management hassles!

# Other Uses of 4☐ in the Language Arts Program

## Book Review

The four square form is an excellent method of preparing the book review paper, starting in even the earliest grades. Using this format is less intimidating when they see it in so many different applications.

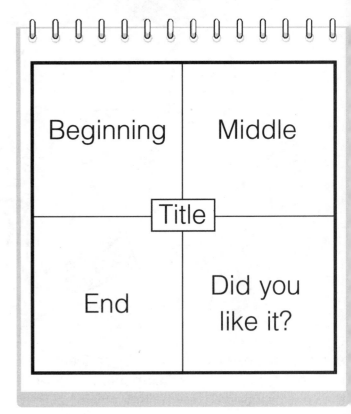

| Beginning | Middle |
|-----------|--------|
| End | Did you like it? |

Title

*The four square book review*

## The 4☐ for Reading Comprehension

Four square can also teach reading comprehension by reading a passage and then building the four square that the writer may have used. One effective way to do this uses the students' own writing. An essay that is well-organized and well-written is prepared on a word processor and printed on heavy-duty paper one sentence at a time. These sentences are then cut up and placed in a can. Each student draws a sentence until none are left. The objective is to reconstruct the story. Students must try to find others with similar topics and details. This is a fun and enriching activity. After the story is re-created and read aloud, the original story can be put on chart paper or overhead transparency. The class then tries to re-create the writer's four square.

## Speeches

Four square, once mastered, is a fabulous method of preparing notes for speeches or debates. It can contain an entire thesis on one page, including some of the specific details and vivid language intended for use. Once trained in writing from the four square, speaking from it will be an easy task.

# 4□ in the Sciences

## Using Four Square as a Study Aid and a Guide to Writing Papers

The four square in the expository form adapts well for the sciences. It serves as an excellent way to review or summarize information learned about a specific topic. Using this method to review can provide the student with all the information that is needed for the essay examination, a more authentic form of assessment.

This basic review-style four square can be expanded and used as the base for a full-length term paper or research paper.

Certainly the occasion will arise when more than three points are made about a topic. Another "box" can be created for other categories of discourse. Once students understand how each box is developed, they will be able to add another box in abstraction.

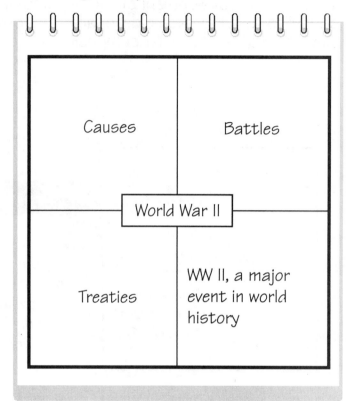

*a four square used in history*

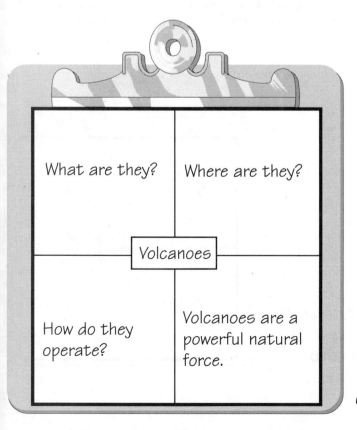

*a four square used in Earth science*

# 4☐ "Within a 4☐"

## Expanding Subtopics for the Longer Composition

To aid in the development of subtopics for the longer paper, students can use the four square to develop each individually. The development of the paper is an easier task if it is viewed as several smaller compositions.

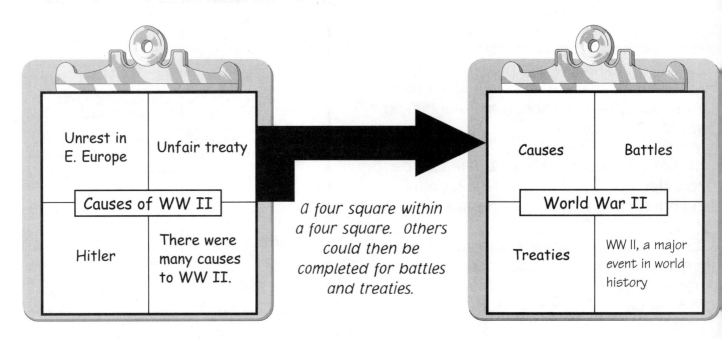

| | |
|---|---|
| Unrest in E. Europe | Unfair treaty |
| **Causes of WW II** | |
| Hitler | There were many causes to WW II. |

*a four square within a four square. Others could then be completed for battles and treaties.*

| | |
|---|---|
| Causes | Battles |
| **World War II** | |
| Treaties | WW II, a major event in world history |

Four square is also an excellent tool for comparing information. Completing similar four squares on contrasting topics gives a clear picture of the similarities and differences.

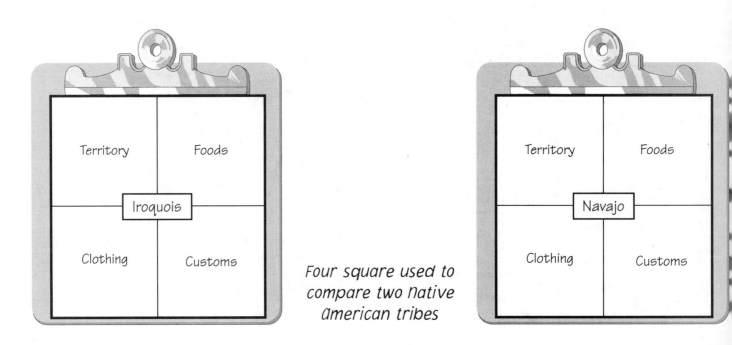

| | |
|---|---|
| Territory | Foods |
| **Iroquois** | |
| Clothing | Customs |

*Four square used to compare two Native American tribes*

| | |
|---|---|
| Territory | Foods |
| **Navajo** | |
| Clothing | Customs |

# 4☐ in Mathematics

## Using Four Square to Organize and Solve Word Problems

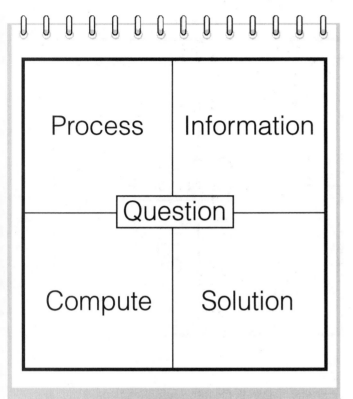

| Process | Information |
|---------|-------------|
| Question | |
| Compute | Solution |

Word problems require the employment of logic and reasoning different from the usual compute and solve drills. These problems require that students develop their own equation and then perform an unnamed operation to find a solution. These steps are not easily completed by the student mathematician.

*a four square using the P.I.C.S. formula for word problems*

The mathematics formula works using a P.I.C.S formula. In the "Process" box the students jot down key words. Certainly lessons will be spent decoding the process for particular question key words. The "Information" box is for the collection of numerical data. In the "Compute" box the problem is written and computed. The "Solution" box is the area where the student places the answer, along with any proper terminology.

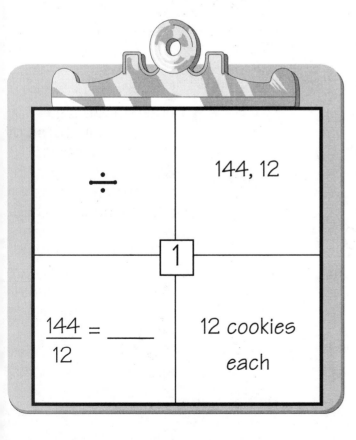

$\div$    144, 12

1

$\dfrac{144}{12} =$ _____    12 cookies each

1. *Susan had baked 144 cookies during the holidays. She wanted to give some to every girl in her scout troop. There are 12 other girls in her troop. How many cookies will each girl get?*

# 4□ in the Arts

## Using Four Square for Art and Music Appreciation

A major part of the art and music curricula in the schools is concerned with teaching the various characteristics in a work and helping students discern between artists or composers. With this knowledge and the ability to distinguish styles, it is more likely that a child will become an educated arts consumer.

In music there are some factors that make for an adequate student analysis. If students can describe and compare the factors of form, harmonization, melody, rhythm and orchestration, they can learn to synthesize this information to render a guess as to the composer or musical era.

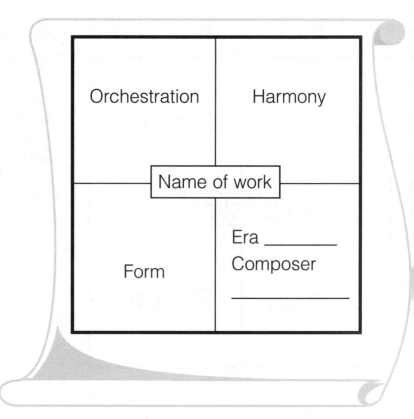

| Orchestration | Harmony |
|---|---|
| Name of work | |
| Form | Era _____ <br> Composer <br> _____ |

*a four square for music style analysis*

Four square also works well in the study of program music. Because these works are musical pieces that tell stories without words, students can use the narrative version of the four square to re-create and write the story being told. Interdisciplinary lessons such as these really make the most of classtime!

# 4▢ in the Arts

## Using Four Square for Art and Music Appreciation

In classroom instruction of the visual arts, a similarly analytical version of the four square can be used. While looking at a new work, students can take notes on a four square on any number of artistic devices and elements. Box 1 would name the work and box 5 would state the artist and era. Learning about art in an organized fashion will enable students to take a more objective look when viewing something new. Hopefully, they won't rush to a judgment without looking at the traits that display the artist's craft.

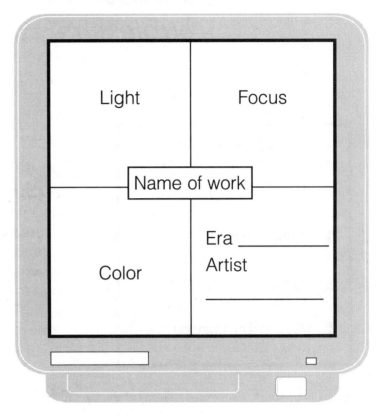

| Light | Focus |
|---|---|
| | Name of work |
| Color | Era _____ Artist _____ |

*a four square for the visual arts style analysis*

# Preparing for a Writing Assessment

## *A Lesson in Reading Those Troublesome Writing Prompts*

### Three Parts to a Prompt

**1.** Who cares?

**2.** Brain activation!

**3.** What to write!

If all we needed to do to enable students to succeed on writing assessments was to teach them good writing practices, our jobs would be simpler. Unfortunately, there is another problem that writers face. The writing test is, in part, a **reading** test. If the writer fails to determine the exact topic and purpose for the essay, even the best organized and most profound writing will not score well.

The information in the writing prompt is usually broken into three parts. In the first part of the prompt the test writers are trying to set up a scene or get the writers into a particular state of mind. They may give a scenario or some background information. This is deemed the "Who cares?" portion of the prompt, for though it may be useful as a scene setter, if writers pay it too much attention, they will likely write off the intended topic.

The second part of a writing prompt usually asks the writer to engage his or her brain to imagine a scenario or recall information. During the reading of this part of the question, the writer **truly needs to think** because the thoughts generated are the seeds for the writing which follows.

The third part of the prompt is the "What to write" portion, because it is there that the prompt usually lists the specifics for the essay and any requirements for its contents. It is recommended that the students <u>underline</u> this portion of the writing prompt because it generally contains the sentence or phrase that will be the center of the four square.

## A Typical Writing Prompt

Travel in a time machine would make it possible to be at any historical event. Imagine that your trip takes you to the signing of the Declaration of Independence. Tell a story about what happens.

## Who cares?

Travel in a time machine would make it possible to be at any historical event.

## Brain activation!

Imagine that your trip takes you to the signing of the Declaration of Independence.

## What to write!

Tell a story about what happens.

In this example the student would write *My Trip to the Signing of the Declaration of Independence* in the center of the four square. Note that the question-writers did *not* want to hear about a time machine alone but only as background information. Recognizing the three parts of the question helps to avoid this error.

In this example the student would write *Why I cherish _____* (object name) in the center of the four square. Note that the question-writers did *not* want to hear about a fire in someone's house but only as background information. Recognizing the three parts of the question helps to avoid this error.

Once students have determined the topic in the essay, they must further determine the requirements for the audience and the purpose for the writing. To teach this the **T.A.P.** acronym works well: **T**opic, **A**udience and **P**urpose.

## T.A.P. Out Those Prompts

**T**opic (goes in your four square center)

**A**udience (information, description, convincing or a story)

**P**urpose (expository, descriptive, persuasive or narrative)

The T.A.P. acronym is a convenient way to remind students to look for the purpose of the essay. They will need to process the question and key in on any words that direct them to the desired purpose of the essay.

| Expository | Persuasive | Descriptive | Narrative |
|---|---|---|---|
| Inform | Convince | Describe | Story |
| Tell steps | Persuade | Senses | Events |
| Explain | | | "Happens" |
| Examples | | | |
| Reasons | | | |

# T.A.P. Those Prompts

*Directions: Read each prompt. Remember the three parts to the prompt. Be sure to underline the "What to write" part. Then complete the topic, audience and purpose for each prompt.*

**1.** Occasionally we find ourselves in a dangerous situation. Think about a time when you had a narrow escape from danger. Tell a story about the experience.

Topic: (Center Box) _____

Audience: (Information, Description, Convincing or Story) _____

Purpose: (Expository, Descriptive, Persuasive or Narrative) _____

**2.** Your school is going to get a new mascot; they need to choose an animal. Think about which animal you would like for the school mascot. Write to convince your principal to choose your mascot.

Topic: (Center Box) _____

Audience: (Information, Description, Convincing or Story) _____

Purpose: (Expository, Descriptive, Persuasive or Narrative) _____

**3.** Everyone has a special place in your home. Where is your special place? Describe the spot in your home that is your favorite.

Topic: (Center Box) _____

Audience: (Information, Description, Convincing or Story) _____

Purpose: (Expository, Descriptive, Persuasive or Narrative) _____

**4.** Children often daydream or fantasize about what they would like their lives to be when they become adults. Hard work and planning can make a dream come true. Think about your goals for the future. Explain to your reader what steps you will take to reach those goals.

Topic: (Center Box) _____

Audience: (Information, Description, Convincing or Story) _____

Purpose: (Expository, Descriptive, Persuasive or Narrative) _____

Name _____

# T.A.P. Those Prompts Answer Key

*Directions: Read each prompt. Remember the three parts to the prompt. Be sure to underline the "What to write" part. Then complete the topic, audience and purpose for each prompt.*

**1.** Occasionally we find ourselves in a dangerous situation. Think about a time when you had a narrow escape from danger. Tell a story about the experience.

Topic: (Center Box) _My narrow escape from danger_

Audience: (Information, Description, Convincing or Story) _Story_

Purpose: (Expository, Descriptive, Persuasive or Narrative) _Narrative_

**2.** Your school is going to get a new mascot; they need to choose an animal. Think about which animal you would like for the school mascot. Write to convince your principal to choose your mascot.

Topic: (Center Box) _I want a guinea pig for our mascot._

Audience: (Information, Description, Convincing or Story) _Convincing_

Purpose: (Expository, Descriptive, Persuasive or Narrative) _Persuasive_

**3.** Everyone has a special place in your home. Where is your special place? Describe the spot in your home that is your favorite.

Topic: (Center Box) _My porch_

Audience: (Information, Description, Convincing or Story) _Description_

Purpose: (Expository, Descriptive, Persuasive or Narrative) _Descriptive_

**4.** Children often daydream or fantasize about what they would like their lives to be when they become adults. Hard work and planning can make a dream come true. Think about your goals for the future. Explain to your reader what steps you will take to reach those goals.

Topic: (Center Box) _I want to be a brain surgeon._

Audience: (Information, Description, Convincing or Story) _Information_

Purpose: (Expository, Descriptive, Persuasive or Narrative) _Expository_

# T.A.P. Those Prompts

*Directions: Read each prompt. Remember the three parts to the prompt. Be sure to underline the "What to write" part. Then complete the topic, audience and purpose for each prompt.*

**1.** The Fountain of Youth is an important historical spot. Imagine that you discovered the Fountain of Youth. Explain how you felt and what happened.

Topic: (Center Box) _____

Audience: (Information, Description, Convincing or Story) _____

Purpose: (Expository, Descriptive, Persuasive or Narrative) _____

**2.** Sometimes when things are lost we must put an ad in a newspaper to help find it. Think about your book bag or knapsack. Describe it for the newspaper ad.

Topic: (Center Box) _____

Audience: (Information, Description, Convincing or Story) _____

Purpose: (Expository, Descriptive, Persuasive or Narrative) _____

**3.** You work hard around your house doing many chores. You keep up your good grades. Think about all the things you do to please your parents. Write to persuade them to give you a bigger allowance.

Topic: (Center Box) _____

Audience: (Information, Description, Convincing or Story) _____

Purpose: (Expository, Descriptive, Persuasive or Narrative) _____

**4.** "A dog is a man's best friend" is an old expression. Think of the ways a dog or other pet is a friend to a particular person. Tell your reader the ways the dog or other pet helps this person. Give reasons and examples.

Topic: (Center Box) _____

Audience: (Information, Description, Convincing or Story) _____

Purpose: (Expository, Descriptive, Persuasive or Narrative) _____

# T.A.P. Those Prompts Answer Key

*Directions: Read each prompt. Remember the three parts to the prompt. Be sure to underline the "What to write" part. Then complete the topic, audience and purpose for each prompt.*

**1.** The Fountain of Youth is an important historical spot. Imagine that you discovered the Fountain of Youth. Explain how you felt and what happened.

Topic: (Center Box) <u>When I discovered the Fountain of Youth</u>

Audience: (Information, Description, Convincing or Story) <u>Story</u>

Purpose: (Expository, Descriptive, Persuasive or Narrative) <u>Narrative</u>

**2.** Sometimes when things are lost we must put an ad in a newspaper to help find it. Think about your book bag or knapsack. Describe it for the newspaper ad.

Topic: (Center Box) <u>My book bag</u>

Audience: (Information, Description, Convincing or Story) <u>Description</u>

Purpose: (Expository, Descriptive, Persuasive or Narrative) <u>Descriptive</u>

**3.** You work hard around your house doing many chores. You keep up your good grades. Think about all the things you do to please your parents. Write to persuade them to give you a bigger allowance.

Topic: (Center Box) <u>I should get a bigger allowance.</u>

Audience: (Information, Description, Convincing or Story) <u>Convincing</u>

Purpose: (Expository, Descriptive, Persuasive or Narrative) <u>Persuasive</u>

**4.** "A dog is a man's best friend" is an old expression. Think of the ways a dog or other pet is a friend to a particular person. Tell your reader the ways the dog or other pet helps this person. Give reasons and examples.

Topic: (Center Box) <u>My dog helps me.</u>

Audience: (Information, Description, Convincing or Story) <u>Information</u>

Purpose: (Expository, Descriptive, Persuasive or Narrative) <u>Expository</u>

# Section 5
# Practice Prompts
## *Expository, Descriptive, Persuasive and Narrative Styles*

Think It!

Plan It!

Write It!

Do It!

Name _____

*Directions: Read the prompt. Identify the "Who cares?" "Brain activation" and "What to write" parts. Underline the "What to write" part.*

You get your first job delivering newspapers. One of the houses on your route is very special. Write a story about your adventures at the house.

# Topic: (Center of your 4☐) _____

_____

# Audience: (Circle one.)

Information          Description          Convincing          Story

# Purpose: (Circle one.)

Expository          Persuasive          Descriptive          Narrative

*Directions: Complete a 4☐ + 3 + C + V*

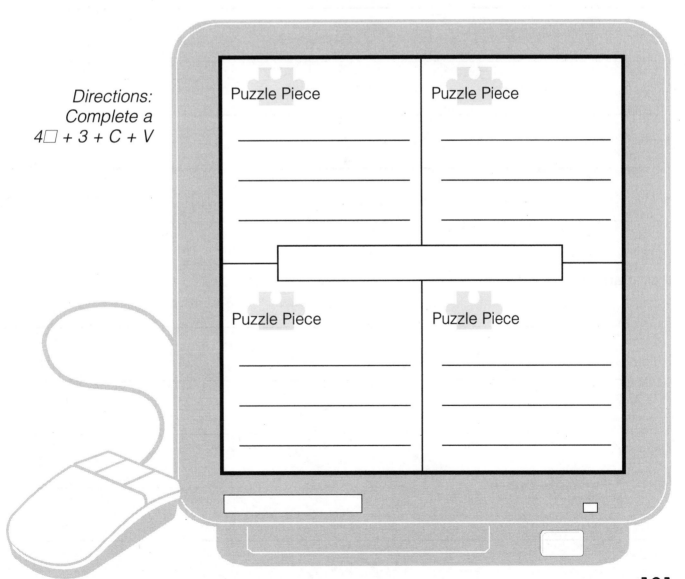

Puzzle Piece

Puzzle Piece

Puzzle Piece

Puzzle Piece

*Directions: Write your story!* Name ______________________

Paragraph 1

Paragraph 2

Paragraph 3

Paragraph 4

_____

_____

_____

_____

Paragraph 5

_____

_____

_____

_____

*Did you indent each paragraph (five times)?*
*Do you have your capitals and periods?*
*Did you write from margin to margin?*
*Did you avoid Tarzan sentences?*

*Directions: Read the prompt. Identify the "Who cares?" "Brain activation" and "What to write" parts. Underline the "What to write" part.*

A local handyman is looking for someone to work for an hour after school to clean his shop and help with some easy chores. Persuade the handyman that you are the best person for this job.

## Topic: (Center of your 4□) _____

_____

## Audience: (Circle one.)

Information          Description          Convincing          Story

## Purpose: (Circle one.)

Expository          Persuasive          Descriptive          Narrative

*Directions: Complete a 4□ + 3 + C + V*

| Puzzle Piece | Puzzle Piece |
|---|---|
| _____ | _____ |
| _____ | _____ |
| _____ | _____ |

| Puzzle Piece | Puzzle Piece |
|---|---|
| _____ | _____ |
| _____ | _____ |
| _____ | _____ |

Paragraph 1

_____

_____

_____

_____

Paragraph 2

_____

_____

_____

_____

Paragraph 3

_____

_____

_____

_____

Paragraph 4

_____

_____

_____

_____

Paragraph 5

_____

_____

_____

_____

*Did you indent each paragraph (five times)?*
*Do you have your capitals and periods?*
*Did you write from margin to margin?*
*Did you avoid Tarzan sentences?*

Name _____

*Directions: Read the prompt. Identify the "Who cares?" "Brain activation" and "What to write" parts. Underline the "What to write" part.*

You are planning a trip around the world. You must choose one way to travel. Think about all the different types of transportation. Which would you choose? Explain why.

# Topic: (Center of your 4☐) _____

_____

# Audience: (Circle one.)

Information          Description          Convincing          Story

# Purpose: (Circle one.)

Expository          Persuasive          Descriptive          Narrative

*Directions: Complete a 4☐ + 3 + C + V*

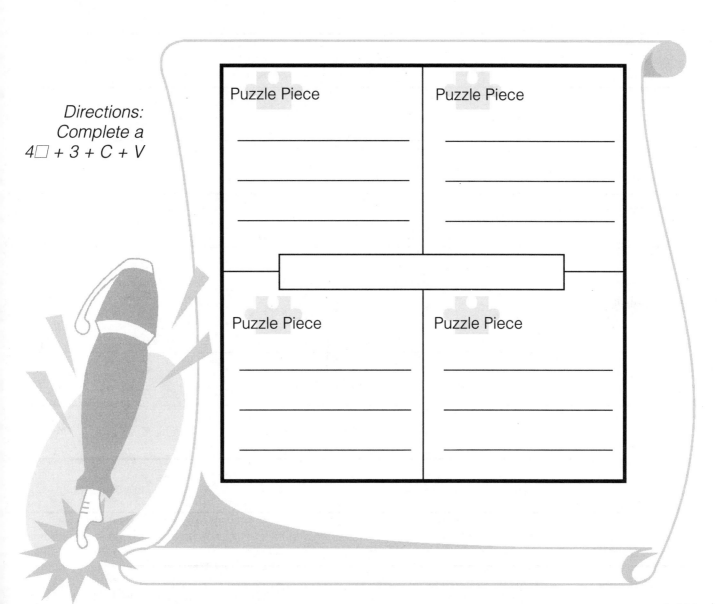

Puzzle Piece

_____

_____

_____

Puzzle Piece

_____

_____

_____

Puzzle Piece

_____

_____

_____

Puzzle Piece

_____

_____

_____

*Directions: Write your story!* Name ______________________

Paragraph 1

______________________________________________

______________________________________________

______________________________________________

______________________________________________

______________________________________________

Paragraph 2

______________________________________________

______________________________________________

______________________________________________

______________________________________________

______________________________________________

Paragraph 3

______________________________________________

______________________________________________

______________________________________________

______________________________________________

______________________________________________

Paragraph 4

_____

_____

_____

_____

Paragraph 5

_____

_____

_____

_____

*Did you indent each paragraph (five times)?*
*Do you have your capitals and periods?*
*Did you write from margin to margin?*
*Did you avoid Tarzan sentences?*

Name _____

*Directions: Read the prompt. Identify the "Who cares?" "Brain activation" and "What to write" parts. Underline the "What to write" part.*

Every teacher has his or her own way of decorating a classroom. Think about the things your teacher has used to decorate. Describe your classroom for your reader. Be sure to include many details.

Topic: (Center of your 4☐) _____

_____

Audience: (Circle one.)

    Information        Description        Convincing        Story

Purpose: (Circle one.)

    Expository        Persuasive        Descriptive        Narrative

*Directions: Complete a 4☐ + 3 + C + V*

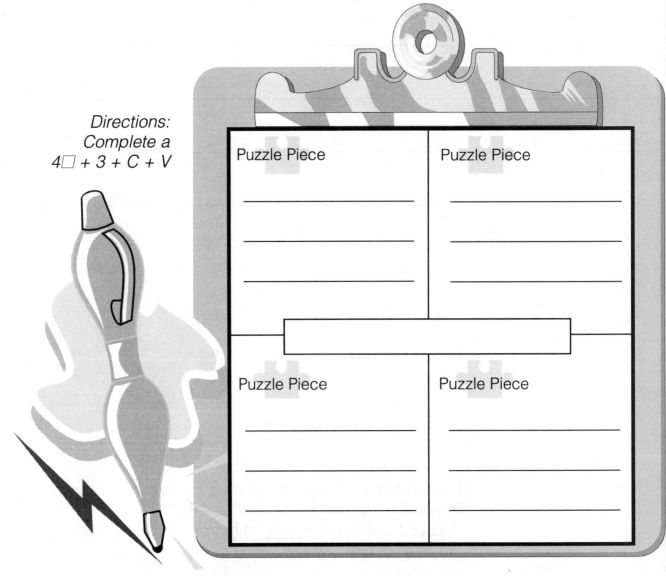

Puzzle Piece

Puzzle Piece

Puzzle Piece

Puzzle Piece

*Directions: Write your story!*  Name _____

Paragraph 1

_____

_____

_____

_____

Paragraph 2

_____

_____

_____

_____

Paragraph 3

_____

_____

_____

_____

Paragraph 4

_____

_____

_____

_____

Paragraph 5

_____

_____

_____

_____

*Did you indent each paragraph (five times)?*
*Do you have your capitals and periods?*
*Did you write from margin to margin?*
*Did you avoid Tarzan sentences?*